JOAN'S WINDOW
on Japan

D1300277

First printing, May 1993

ISBN 0-9696565-1-3

Editorial Consultant
Paul V. Gopal

Published by
JP Publishing
1465 Morley Blvd.
Ottawa, Ontario
K2C 1R4 Canada

Printed in Canada

Joan's window on Japan

A drip-dry Canadian
and other across-the-Pacific tales

Joan Kabayama

Illustrated by Jack Nakamoto

TO MY CHILDREN:

Maki
Noreen
Lawrence
Allison
and
Allen

Preface

When I came across *Joan's Window* in the *Daily Yomiuri* about five years ago I was a bit surprised. I had first met Mrs. Joan Kabayama some years earlier when she was visiting my hometown, Chichibu city, near Tokyo. I have enjoyed talking with her several times since then, but never thought that I would see her opinions in a Japanese newspaper.

The writings of her column interested me so much that I began to cut them out and paste them in a notebook. The notebook now contains a number of articles with topics ranging from everyday things to international issues. They are all based on Mrs.Kabayama's own experiences or observations.

It seems to me that *Joan's Window* has two intentions. One is to promote cross-cultural understanding. The other is to affirm the equality of all human beings, entirely apart from sex, race, and nationality. As citizens living in an age of internationalization, we need to ponder these two themes more deeply

5

and develop minds free from prejudice and preconception.

In her well-written articles Mrs. Kabayama often draws comparisons between Japanese customs and manners, and those of the West, particularly the United States and Canada. Her thoughtful insight into different cultures can be greatly instructive when we attempt to understand other cultures.

I have been looking forward to the publication of *Joan's Window* in book form for a long time, and am delighted to see that this cherished project is finally being realized.

Masami Fujita
Elementary School Principal
Saitama, Japan

February 1993

Joan heads for Japan

A T an age when most people start to take life easier, former Carleton Board of Education trustee and community activist Joan Kabayama is tackling a new career challenge – teaching in Japan.

On the eve of departure, 57-year-old Kabayama's greatest challenge Wednesday was sorting through the jumble of half packed cartons in her Nepean dining room to squeeze her incredibly full life into one suitcase and a box. The veteran school trustee, a champion of rights of minorities, women and the disabled, has taken a two-year contract to teach English at the Tokyo YWCA College.

She has sold her house, divided her belongings among her five children and taken a leave of absence from her job of 19 years as a career and guidance counsellor at Nepean High School.

As well as teaching English, Kabayama will be offering career counselling to young Japanese women. She's hoping to stay on at the college as a full-time career counsellor when her term expires, and says she may retire in the country where her ex-husband was born.

Challenges are her life.

She was born with scoliosis, a crippling congenital curvature of the spine.

But instead of allowing the disease to get worse, Kabayama took to swimming with a vengeance, using the pools at the YM-YWCA in Montreal, where she was brought up.

In 1948 and 1949, Kabayama was on the national swim team and won four medals during Olympic trials. She continues to swim daily and has been a swimming and water-polo coach for local high school teams since 1967.

Kabayama says her aquatic therapy kept her from surgery until two years ago. She was bedridden for six months while recovering from an operation in which rods were put in her spine to straighten the crumpled vertebrae.

Even then, the energetic Kabayama used her time taking an art correspondence course and championing her favourite cause at that time – handicapped people's rights – by writing letters to politicians.

Kabayama, a single parent since 1973, ran as an NDP candidate in 1972 and 1974 against Walter Baker in the federal Grenville-Carleton riding.

She was elected to the Carleton Board of Education, where she served for 13 years (1972 - 1985).

Extracted from
The Ottawa Citizen
May 1, 1986

Equal pay,
a non-starter

The chief obstacle to the implementation of Japan's May 1986 Equal Employment Opportunity Law is that there is no concept in Japan of equal pay for equal work even among men, and without such a fundamental concept it is impossible to extend equal opportunity to women.

Let me explain.

In Japan there is no such thing as a salary scale, which North Americans take for granted in their collective agreements or contracts. In North America, a skilled occupation, in which experience is an important element, may have approximately 10 substantial annual increments, after which the salary remains fairly level (at about twice the starting salary except for across-the-board cost-of-living adjustments.)

A less skilled job would have fewer levels in its salary scale, you would reach your maximum sooner.

Your only substantial increase thereafter

would be as a result of a promotion, or a very large negotiated increment for all employees.

In Japan this concept is totally foreign. Here your salary depends on what your starting pay happened to be the year you were hired, and the increments appear to be automatic every year as long as you stay with your employer.

Under the lifetime employment system enjoyed by civil servants and employees of large companies this means that there can be some almost totally unproductive staff earning substantially more than more productive colleagues who just haven't been around for as long.

It also means that anyone who is out of the work force for a lengthy period due to illness or for further study can never catch up in pay to a colleague the same age.

This is a special handicap for women who take maternity leave. This is the key issue which must be addressed if equal pay for equal work is ever to be accomplished in Japan.

Flying
a lead balloon

I continue to be surprised, puzzled and disappointed here in Japan, over the long and seemingly unnecessary delays which take place between the time administrative decisions are made, and the time they are implemented.

Let me give just a few examples.

A few years ago the report of the Ad Hoc Education Reform Council received Cabinet-level approval. Among the recommendations to be adopted is a change to a five-day school week. Isn't it odd that the government recognizes this as an important change, but asks that implementation be delayed for **over five years**? By that time every child currently in elementary school will have advanced to middle school, and those now enroled in high school will **never** benefit from the change.

More recently, local government officials across the country agreed that their offices should close on Saturdays to give their employees a five-day week. They stated, however, that this change could not be implemented for four or five years, as it would take that long to notify everyone.

This excuse would make sense if Japan were not such a highly literate country, or if we had not yet reached the age of mass communication. Notice of such a change could be printed on, or enclosed with the next annual resident tax bill.

The newspapers would probably give it free coverage on the front page, with headlines. If all else failed, a notice could be posted on the door of each municipal building, and the news would travel very quickly indeed.

Perhaps they're just floating a trial balloon to test community reaction.

Since such a change would most seriously inconvenience foreign residents, who need to renew their alien registrations in person, perhaps they ought to consider either giving some staff Saturdays off, and the others Mondays. Another possibility would be to stay open only one Saturday per month to handle such problems.

A third example of administrative inertia may be found in the courts, when a conviction has been obtained based upon a forced confession alone, and the confession has subsequently been retracted. It may take 10, 20, or 30 years for a retrial to be granted and the person released. Some innocent people have spent more than half their lives in jail, and some have died while awaiting retrial. Delayed justice is no justice at all.

If a decision is worth making, its implementation should not be delayed beyond a year.

Baggy pants

Nearly ten years ago when my son and I stepped off the plane in Japan, his first comment was about the clothing styles.

He wondered aloud, "Why do Japanese young people wear baggy pants?" His answer came very soon, during our first visit to a private home.

Kneeling on the floor around a low table, he found was not very comfortable in straight cut jeans. In fact, one's circulation was cut off, and getting up again became quite painful. There was a very practical reason for this fashion.

I'm a drip-dry Canadian

W hen I first arrived here in Japan in May 1986, it happened to be just a few days after the Chernobyl nuclear accident. On my second Sunday here, I set out for church in a light rain, wearing my raincoat, but carrying no umbrella.

Since I usually have books and other gear with me, I find I have no hand free to carry one. I got part-way down the block, and a lady who was out walking her dog, insisted that I take her umbrella, even though she and I didn't speak each other's language, and she knew that I didn't know where she lived to return it later. My first thought was that she was concerned about the radioactive rain, which had by then been identified. Japanese, having experienced radioactive rain, I thought would be especially sensitive and worried about the matter.

Now, however, nearly a year later, I have come to realize that the Japanese are inordinately worried about becoming wet. We have

had a few light snowfalls this winter, and in response, out come the umbrellas.

This creates a particular problem on rainy week-day mornings. In this city of approximately 12 million people, nearly 8 million ride the subway, and the local train network. There are no school buses here, so all the school children are on, as well as the working people.

Can you picture eight million damp people and eight million wet umbrellas struggling for space on the already sardine-packed system? I wish that school hours were staggered so that children, for their own safety, didn't have to ride during rush hour.

I recall that we started school at 9:30 a.m. in Montreal for a few years when I was in school, and the public transportation system was overloaded, and it seemed to help. Also I wish these children's parents were more thoughtful of others, and dressed them in raincoats and rainhats. With their umbrellas open, these little ones cannot see where they are going, and are a real menace on the narrow sidewalk.

When my friends here try to insist that I share the shelter of their umbrella, I tell them, "It's quite alright. Please look after yourself. I'm drip-dry."

And I thought you were selfish...

It is so easy to have one's motives misunderstood in another culture. For example, the younger son of the family with whom I did my first homestay in Japan, told me a year later, and after three further homestay visits, that his first impression of me was that I was selfish. The incident that had caused this took place on my first day in their home.

I was invited to sit at the kitchen table and a plate containing a Nashi, or Japanese pear, was placed in front of me, along with a small fork. I assumed that they had already eaten theirs, and proceeded to eat it all myself. I soon learned, however, that in Japan fruit is so expensive that usually one is served only half an orange or half a banana, and only a quarter of a large apple. The Nashi, the size of quite a large apple, was meant to be shared among the entire family.

Although I was not hungry I ate the fruit to be polite, but they thought I was being rude.

Questionable equality

I had the pleasure of spending the summer as a graduate student at Sophia University in Tokyo. One day, as we were returning to the city as a group, our bus passed an object which had an unforgettable, distressing impact upon me.

First, I must explain that over 20 years ago I had participated in the march on Washington led by Martin Luther King. Up to that time black Americans were expected to fight and die for their country, but could be shot dead at home just trying to register to place their names on the voters' lists, not to speak of actually voting!

I personally find revolting any exploitation of other human beings, male or female, old or young, of any colour. The offending item was a huge bill-board depicting the back of a naked kneeling female, wearing a leather collar and a heavy chain hanging down her back.

It was not the woman's nakedness that was offensive. Surely I, as a coach for nearly 20 years of young men's and women's swimming and waterpolo teams, and quite accustomed to various degrees of undress, am not easily offended by the human body.

Before writing I discussed this thoroughly with my older, married son, and we both agreed that whether the person in the advertisement were male or female, naked or fully clothed, it is the subservient position with the collar and chain that makes it repulsive.

It is not humorous and it is not trivial. In fact it makes us question just how deeply social equality, as a measure of democracy, has been accepted into Japanese society.

Alone in Tokyo, afraid to be sick

A friend of mine, a university lecturer, has been seriously ill in a Tokyo municipal hospital for several months.

In spite of having the best medical insurance in the country ... the kind that pays 90 percent of hospital costs ... her experience has been frightening.

During the first three months in hospital, her "overbilling" amounted to **six months' salary**.

After another three months she lost her home.

No matter how excellent the level of medical care is, and I, myself, have been well cared for as an outpatient here, such heavy financial anxiety must surely interfere with recovery.

The only other industrialized country with which I am familiar that this could happen in is the United States.

There I have heard of patients being forced to sign a cheque for the anaesthetist as they were being wheeled into the operating room. In some cases others have been left to die on the hospital steps because they had no insurance.

Japanese readers may be interested to know that even before "overbilling" became illegal in Canada most doctors did not charge more than the insurance would cover.

Five years ago I had extensive spinal surgery, requiring over three weeks' hospitalization, and was not "overbilled" by one cent. Not one yen, even.

When I came here seven years ago leaving my two youngest children at universities in Canada they were provided with free full medical coverage. Yet our taxes are about the same.

If you have never been afraid to be sick, you have no concept of how important such a sense of security is.

I believe Japan chose the wrong country as a model for its health delivery services.

Greener grasses

Is the grass on the other side of the fence really greener? How many times have you heard people compare their own country's culture unfavourably with that of another?

There are some reasons for this belief, although in most cases it is a false assumption.

Let me give you a few examples.

This fall there will be a splendid exhibition of examples of Samurai artifacts and museum pieces on display in Washington. Last September there was a two-week Japanese cultural fair in Ottawa, featuring music and films by some of Japan's leading film makers.

The materials for these exhibits or cultural festivals are carefully selected, and represent some of the finest of Japanese culture. As a result, many North Americans feel that the cultural level in Japan is somehow higher than their own.

Some foreigners are quite devastated, when they have been in Japan for a while, to find that most Japanese movies are not of the level of quality they expected. In fact, one small city of seventy or eighty thousand people has only two theatres and the residents complain that they show only horror or pornographic films.

A national survey conducted by the Japanese government last year showed that of all people 15 years old or over, only a third had gone to movies during the past year.

This is partly due to the ticket price (three or four times the cost in North America) but also partly due to the poor quality, if you do not happen to be in a large city with a wide variety of films showing.

Because the accessibility to cultural activities is not as good in Japan as in North America, due to the high cost, and also because of the comparative lack of leisure time, the level of cultural enjoyment is actually lower.

Japanese also suffer from the "greener pastures" syndrome. When I first came to Japan in 1984, I was studying in the city of Chichibu, Saitama-ken, a city famous for its wine. My host went out and bought a bottle of French wine for dinner, something I could have had at less than half the price at home. What I really wanted was to sample the famous wine from that area of Japan.

It really distresses me when people downgrade their own culture, or even reject it in favour of that of some other country. That is surely not the essence of internationalism.

Fair exchange

Not everything cultural can be found in art galleries, museums or theaters. When excavations were made of the civilization of the Roman Empire, particular attention and admiration centred around the Roman plumbing system and the Roman baths.

According to the 1985 census, only 58 percent of Japanese private homes had flush toilets. The rest still employed "outhouses," not unlike the rural areas of North America only a generation ago.

Japanese flush toilets come in two types, as you will no doubt have discovered. As in many countries of Eastern Europe, the Japanese-style toilet is a ceramic hole in the floor, requiring a degree of gymnastic talent which is beyond the mastery of most older Westerners. They are also not convenient for the handicapped or for anyone wearing complicated clothing.

There are several features of Japanese

"Western" toilets which I feel are very deserving of adoption elsewhere. Many North American cities suffer from chronic water shortages and would benefit greatly from the choice of a small-flush or a large-flush, a characteristic of all Japanese flush toilets. In North America in an effort to save water, we place two building bricks in the water reservoir, and as a result we can only get a "small" flush.

A second admirable feature is the way the back of most toilets is shaped like a small hand-basin, into which clean water arches which can be used for hand washing, before it refills the reservoir. I was raised in Montreal, and have lived in a private home in Amsterdam, in both of which it was common for the toilet to be in a separate room from the wash basin, tub or shower. This hand washing feature would have been much appreciated.

The *piece de resistance,* however, has to be the delightful custom in modern private homes of having an electrically heated toilet seat.

The electrical outlet in the wall beside the toilet permits it to be plugged in, in cold weather, much as we in North America can plug in our car's block heaters on a cold night. This feature, which permits homes to be kept at a significantly cooler night temperature, and with energy savings besides, is one I really appreciate here in the winter.

When I spent my Christmas holidays in Hokkaido, with friends who had to leave their car running for many minutes before driving it, I was surprised to find that they hadn't heard of block heaters for cars.

I told my hosts I would be prepared to trade a block heater for a plug-in-toilet seat. This is one kind of cultural exchange that can make life more enjoyable for us all.

Telephone hurdles

The biggest frustration in my life involves the Japanese telephone... starting with the "phone directory." I can't use it because it's not in our Roman alphabet, but it is in the old classical Chinese characters or Kanji, and there are many symbols which sound the same.

For example to look up our name, Kabayama, you would have to know whether we are the *Kaba* that means "birch trees" (we are) or the *Kaba* that means "water buffalo." Then you would need the symbols, or Kanji, for the given name of the family member in whose name the phone was listed. On top of that there are so many listings that they don't list the complete address, only the district. When I first came I tried to find the number of a friend who was one of 240 of the same family name and had two ways to represent his given name.

It was like trying to guess which Joan Kabayama I was if there were a great many in

the Ottawa area, and the address was listed as Nepean. It's almost like having an unlisted number.

Then there's the matter of financing these calls.

Pay phones give you a certain number of seconds per 10-yen coin (about $0.10) and if you run over, or there is something wrong with the phone, you get cut off. Some phones take 100-yen coins also (about $1.00) and these are devoured in the same way for long distance calls.

I cannot telephone home to Canada, not because of the cost ($30 or $40), but because of the stack of change I would need to keep feeding into the telephone.

Local calls on private phones are also charged by time. I hope we **never** fall victim to paying by the minute for local calls in Canada.

It makes one hesitate to use a friend's phone and to avoid using the office phone for even the most urgent personal call. In the city we write to each other.

Them, not us

While watching the World Figure Skating championships on NHK-TV in Tokyo, I became really angry at a not-too-subtle form of discrimination.

When the Japanese skater Midori Ito appeared, her name was flashed on the screen in correct Japanese Kanji. When the Japanese-American skater Kristi Yamaguchi performed, however, her entire name was displayed in Katakana, the phonetic script used to aid in the pronunciation of foreign or "borrowed" words.

Yamaguchi is one of the simplest of Japanese family names and would be recognizable by most primary school children. It was the TV station's way of drawing attention to the fact that the Yamaguchi girl was not a "real" Japanese.

I was really insulted on Miss Yamaguchi's behalf, and wrote to tell the TV station how I felt. I received no answer.

I was sufficiently upset to tell my Japanese language teacher about it, but she only looked at me in astonishment, and asked, "Don't you think we Japanese have the right to decide who is Japanese, and who isn't?"

She clearly missed my point that this was a totally unnecessary and pernicious form of discrimination. Being Japanese or non-Japanese has little to do with the use of Kanji. My teacher and others have forgotten that Kanji are not the exclusive property of the Japanese.

By contrast, in the case of professional entertainers from China, the Japanese media seem to use Kanji at the option of the individual. For example, Theresa Teng chooses to write her name in Katakana, while Oh Yang Fifi chooses Kanji to write her name, but keeping the Chinese pronunciation.

In Japanese or Chinese, the correct Kanji are part of the spelling of your name. If someone used the wrong Kanji to write your name, even if it had the identical sound, you would correct him, just as we would in English, if someone wrote "two" instead of "too." To insist on using Kanji with some Japanese names and Katakana with others is a pointless distinction, an artificial convention.

You can imagine how pleased I am, that the two Japanese publications for which I write do me the courtesy of printing my family name in Kanji.

Packing for overseas stay

One Friday evening my best friend in Tokyo brought a class mate from her German class over to meet me. Her friend had won a scholarship for a year's study in Germany, and wanted my advice about what to take.

My friend knew that I had once gone to Holland to summer school with only two shoulder-bags: my purse (large) and a C.P. Air bag. She felt I was an expert on travelling light.

My advice to her was to take one or two nylon flight bags, because they weigh almost nothing when empty. I suggested that she be completely packed a month in advance, and that if she found anything in that last month that she absolutely must take, then something else had to be left out!

If she needed any prescription medicines, she should take them with her, but for vitamins and any other pharmaceuticals, she could get them cheaper in any other country, as Japan has to be most expensive country for vitamins and food supplements!

Books are a no-no, especially hard-covered ones. When I came to Japan I brought only six paperbacks: *Black Like Me* (John Howard Griffin); *The Prophet* (Kahil Gibran); *Essays by Henri Poincare* (Dover Press); *Political Women in Japan* (a gift from my older son before I left) and two books of poetry.

My room looks like a typical student room, decorated with 13 laminated posters from Canada, including the Carleton Board affirmative action poster, the Takahashi Dojo Poster (my children's judo school in Ottawa) and the front page of *The Clarion* - the issue with my oldest daughter's picture on it, when she joined the National Ballet Company. All 13 posters came rolled up in a single mailing tube, light and unbreakable, and important mementos of home.

Our baggage mustn't become a burden!

A persistent shame

A Japanese friend of mine is upset, ashamed and angry that prostitution still flourishes in Japan, more that 30 years after the passage of the Anti-Prostitution Law. This law was part of the process of Japan's becoming an acceptable world citizen, before being admitted to membership of the United Nations. Some call it a "cosmetic" law.

My friend points out that now that we have the Equal Employment Opportunity Law and a comparatively high national average income level, there is no excuse for such activity. If the causes were purely economic, then he would be absolutely correct. The strict enforcement of the letter and spirit of the equal employment law would make the problem soon disappear all on its own.

Unfortunately there are other aspects of the problem which must be addressed, before any significant progress will be made. The first is legislative. The government will have to come to terms with the fact that nearly two-thirds of its citizens feel strongly that prostitution must be prevented, and move swiftly to close the legal loopholes which permit soaplands and similar establishments to operate.

A second aspect is an educational one.

It is quite evident that the Education Ministry's curriculum for both moral educational and sex education have been, with a few shining exceptions, a colossal failure.

To support this educational program to promote self respect, we need to have a look at an important area of this society which creates widespread and flagrant offense against women. That is the combination of violence and pornography which abounds even in so-called "comic books," or *manga*, for teenagers. For starters, perhaps the Japanese government might like to study the West German government's attitude toward pornography.

Humorously, it appears that some of them have already encountered it! On an expedition to West Germany only a few years ago, a member of then-Prime Minister Yasuhiro Nakasone's entourage committed a faux pas in a magazine shop. He reportedly opened the plastic wrapper and began flipping through the magazine right there in the shop, completely unaware of the local laws. The magazine shop owner went over to him, snatched the magazine away and slapped his hand.

In West Germany, if you buy a pornographic magazine, you must take it home and break the seal in the privacy of your own home. If you want to rot your brains (you don't have to believe in an immoral soul) you must do it in private, so as not to offend others.

This type of law would at least remove one major source of offense-the ill mannered, gross displays on subways and trains, without regard to the sensitivities of women and some men. If women are to have self-respect, it must be in cooperation with men. It cannot be done unilaterally.

Finally, how do we help those women who have become involved, for one reason or another, in prostitution? The problem is very great. It isn't completely solved when the woman has been rescued, if necessary, from criminal control and helped to gain a new evaluation of herself. Then comes the job interview. When the interviewer looks over her rather sparse employment history, looks at her and asks: "And what kind of work have you been doing for the past 10 years?" How does she answer?

Grocery store discipline

J ust before I came to Tokyo, I read an article describing this city as the most expensive in the world. Certainly the rents (similar to New York but for much smaller accommodation) and entertainment costs (fourteen or fifteen dollars for a movie that would cost four or five dollars in Canada) leave little for luxuries.

It is in the grocery store that the shopper must exercise great talent and self-discipline. Staples such as bread and dairy products are not subsidized here, and for about $1.75 I can have my choice among one of: a litre of milk, or a 500g container of plain yogurt or a very small container of cottage cheese (the size of an individual yogurt). A loaf of white bread is about the same price. Rice, the main staple for Japanese families, costs six to ten times the world price, because imports are restricted and priced equally high, so as not to compete with the locally-grown, uneconomically produced product.

You may have read recently about the economic rice wars being fought between the U.S and Japan. The cost of this battle is borne by the Japanese consumer. Similarly beef prices are kept high to match local unprofitable cattle-raising costs, so that here we pay about the same for 100 grams that we would pay for a kilogram in Canada. It's a good thing I like fish.

Fruit prices are also out-of-sight. For example a musk melon or honeydew melon here will cost from 800 to 1200 yen, or from eight to twelve dollars each, depending on size at a time when they are being advertised in the Ottawa and Toronto area for 79 to 99 cents each. A very small watermelon could cost fifteen dollars. Melons are bought as gifts, rather than for personal use. All fruit is expensive, such that if we have fruit for breakfast, we will be served half a banana or half a pear per person or a quarter of a large apple. Oranges that left California at 40 cents a pound, will reach $9 a pound before meeting the consumer. The many-staged distribution system here seems to result in a doubling of price at each level of handling.

I often think of the Boston Tea Party and its political consequences, and feel that Japan is ready, in particular, for a Tokyo Rice Party. Consumers here are not accustomed to boycotting high-priced items.

Toilet slippers

After my first summer in Japan I was asked by some Japanese friends, what I found to be most funny or strange in Japan. It had to be toilet slippers!

At the conference centre where we stayed, there was a large bathroom on each floor, with about 20 cubicle-enclosed units, and at least that many pairs of slippers, all plainly marked "toilet slipper," at the door.

This can lead to some embarrassing moments, as one member of our party went down to an informal evening reception in our building, and looked down to find she was still wearing the "toilet slippers." I have made the same mistake in a private home.

Originally, as in Canada, such facilities were outhouses, and in fact as late as 1985, as many as seventy pre cent of homes across Japan still did not have indoor toilets, and this place was not considered clean enough to enter in your sock feet.

Most Japanese homes, however, are spotlessly clean, and in nine years I have only found one in which I felt it was really neces-

found one in which I felt it was really necessary to put on their toilet slippers. Like most customs, everywhere, it arose from a genuine need, but it lingers on to this day in almost every home.

The one advantage is that if you are wearing house slippers and you leave yours **outside** the bathroom when you enter, it allows others to see at once if that facility is "occupied."

42

Space-age toilet attack

L ast summer a Canadian friend, a lady in her 70's, attended a conference in Tokyo. The conference arrangements included a home stay.

All went well until she went to use the bathroom. On the wall, beside the toilet was hung a handwritten notice that read: *For man push button #--* and *For lady push button #--*. No mention was made of remaining seated. Consequently when my friend finished using the toilet, she stood up, leaned over, found the right button and pushed.

To her astonishment she was showered with warm water from head to foot, and over a good part of the floor. She hastily put the cover down, took a towel and mopped up herself and the floor as well as she could before going down to dinner. Since neither she nor her host family ever referred to the incident again, I wonder if they ever did realize the inadequacy of their instructions?

Counselling differences

There is a significant difference which I observed between Japan and North America, in both the methods and goals of counselling.

In Canada and the United States, in three provinces and two states over a period of thirty years, my role as a counsellor was three-fold. First, it was to help the client to clarify the problem itself.

Then we identified as many as possible of the possible choices of action, along with the likely results of making each of the choices.

I would say, "Based on my observation and experience, if you make choice A, this is the probable consequence, if you make choice B, I believe that will happen." And so on. Then I would suggest to the counselee that he/she go and think it over for a few days, getting the reactions of any others whose opinions were respected, such as parents or close friends.

Finally, we would meet again for the counselee to tell ME which decision had been cho-

sen and whether my help was needed to accomplish it. In other word, the goal was to help that person gain control over his or her life and be better able to solve future problems.

Even in the case of a pregnant high school student, after we had reviewed her options, I would say, "Your parents will have to know. Can you tell them yourself, or do you want me to tell them? Or, shall we tell them together?"

That implies that the person whose life and whose problem it is should remain, as much as possible, in control and with a feeling of control. Here in Japan the client's expectations are very different. Here I am expected to come up with one plan or solution, and even to give the counselee a firm nudge in that direction. The Japanese counselee seems only to want a means of coping with the current crisis. There is little concept of looking ahead to the direction one's life is taking, or of developing decision making skills.

Some of my counselees in Japan have looked at me with obvious disappointment, and said, "Aren't you going to tell me what to do?" These cultural differences in expectations can lead to a lack of confidence between Japanese and those of us who were raised elsewhere.

Driving in opposite directions

In North America as well as in Japan we are concerned about the safety of our young people, and are equally anxious about the traffic accident rates among young men in particular, since young women appear to be as safe drivers as adults.

Our approach to solving this problem, however, is diametrically opposite. In North America we set up after school "driver education" courses, which we are able to offer at about half the cost of commercial driving schools, or of the order of $250 instead of $500. Presumably part of the cost saving is due to using school buildings and property, but also I believe we are willing to subsidize this program out of concern for our children's safety. The fact that these educational programs are successful is reflected in the willingness of car insurance companies to issue reduced-price insurance premiums to these graduates, because their records show that such young people have as good driving safety as the average adult.

In Japan the approach is quite the opposite. Thirty-one of Japan's prefectures, including over 80 percent of Japanese high schools, have regulations which require the expulsion of any student who obtains a driver's license or who either owns or uses a motorbike.

In other words, the effort is directed toward preventing youths from driving, rather than to help them to do it safely.

Isn't this an interesting example of how our cultural differences lead us to completely opposite solutions to the same problem?

In North America and Australia, although we know it is not mandatory, many people, especially city dwellers, do prepare for their license test by attending driving schools.

To me it remains a source of amazement that any Japanese holds a driver's license, considering the cost. In the first place, almost everyone in Japan believes it is a legal requirement to pass through a commercial driving school, where the minimum cost is over Y100,000 ($1,000 Cdn.) and includes two paper tests and two road tests.

Moreover, most people do not pass with only the minimum hours of road instruction. This is in contrast to corresponding courses in North America, in which a majority do pass after the minimum number of hours of practical work. In Japan, driving is another luxury.

Different
priorities

Every time I hear the U.S. government applying pressure on the Japanese government to increase defense spending I get angry. Surely they would not do this if they had any idea that in Japan high school education is not yet free.

My friends in North America are shocked to find out that parents in Japan must pay as much or more to send their children to high school as North Americans pay to send their children to university.

For example, at the lower extreme, a Tokyo metropolitan high school costs Y7,440 per month plus a small entrance fee. There is also a "school excursion" fee of Y8,200 per month toward the graduation class trip.

The upper end of the range, is represented by a good private high school whose fees are Y360,000 per year, with a one-time admission fee of Y350,000.

There are additional expenses such as a monthly instalment toward their graduation

49

trip. A few cost even more. One of my friends estimates that Y600,000 or about $6,000 a year is about average.

Most Japanese families must allocate about 25 percent of their income to their children's education, either current or future.

As a result, the typical middle-class family has its "back against the wall" financially, and can afford little in the way of the luxuries that we in North America take for granted, such as the occasional movie or concert.

Surely the United States government would not want a friendly ally to put more money into defense when it cannot even afford to provide free high school education for its youth.

In principle, no country should be spending a significant military sum without first attending to its citizens' educational and medical needs, although many Third World countries regrettably do so.

Japan should continue to serve as a model to other nations of the way in which an economy can thrive when it does not devote its human and material resources to non-productive uses.

Fastfood tiers

In Japan you can find three fairly distinct grades of fast food establishments at similar prices.

A typical first class fast food restaurant, in the neighbourhood of my college, is exemplified by a fine *sushi* bar where excellent fresh *sushi* is being prepared continuously, and placed on a kind of moving track that resembles a child's train track. The chef or chefs are on the inside of the track. The patrons, on bar stools at the counter on the outside of the track, help themselves as their favourite dishes go by.

You are charged by the plate, when you have finished. All the plates cost the same (120 yen or a little over a dollar) and the restaurant serves from two pieces for the more expensive ingredients such as shrimp or salmon, to six for the smaller less expensive vegetable *sushi* per plate.

It is one of the few real bargains I have found in Japan. My favourite place serves a

51

wide variety, including three kinds of shrimp. There is almost always a lineup to be served.

The middle class fast meal is served at a corner, stand-up counter where *soba,* or noodles, hot or cold, and with various toppings, constitute the menu. These are also well attended, and the meals are tasty, costing 400 or 500 yen, or as much as four or five plates of *sushi.*

For many years there were only two classes of fast food, but in recent years there has been a rapid proliferation of a third, and lower level. These are the hamburger outlets whose products are smaller, limper and more tasteless than their North American counterparts. They are also more expensive.

When they don't have a special sale price war on, you could be charged almost 700 yen (about $7.00) for the minimum lunch... burger, fries and drink, making these places also the least value for your money. High pressure advertising, however, has made them popular hang-outs for the young.

An open and
shut case

One summer I was certain that the Japanese teacher in the next room was determined to kill me. That was the year that we had to teach right through the summer months, and Tokyo was suffering from both extreme heat and a severe water shortage.

Our dormitory was not air conditioned. Water was so short that on Thursdays we could neither bathe nor do laundry.

The only way we could get to sleep at all was to try to get a cross draught. By leaving the French doors to my fire escape open on the south side and by leaving my room door and the hall window open on the north side, it was possible to get a bit of air.

This seemed to bother my neighbour, who got up around 2 a.m. and quietly closed the hall window. By 3 a.m. I was wide awake, closely resembling a human stew, and had to get up quietly and reopen the window in order to get back to sleep.

It appears she had a fear of "peeping toms" and prowlers, even though our building was surrounded by a stone wall. If she had come in and sat on the side of my bed she would have realized that the only view from there was a neighbour's red brick wall.

Of course, she was not aware of the Canadian custom of being sure that one's bedroom windows are always open at night, and that some of us even do this in the middle of winter, to keep a circulation of fresh air.

I can never read Abe's *Woman In The Dunes* without recalling vividly that summer's ordeal.

Return to sender

I hope that the Japan Chamber of Commerce and Industry and the Tokyo Chamber of Commerce and Industry will take note of this problem. and exert pressure until it is remedied. For a modern, industrialized country too much mail is being lost.

This applies to mail addressed in Japanese as well as in English. Let me share a few people's experiences.

For a few months last spring, my son was here, staying with one of my male colleagues, who has lived in the same apartment in Japan for several years. Two letters were mailed to my son. One was a "special delivery" containing a map. Both were sent back to their senders stamped "undeliverable." The postman did not try to deliver them. He just did not know my son and assumed he did not exist.

A year ago a Japanese businessman in Tokyo should have received an important envelope from Brazil. He owns his own business and operates out of one office in a downtown building. The envelope was correctly addressed in every respect. There was no cause for confusion. His postal carrier, however, stamped it "undeliverable" and returned it to Brazil. Fortunately, the Brazilian company representative made a long-distance call and the business transaction was made, with no help from the Japanese postal service.

Last summer, an Australian teacher (working in Japan) took a group of college students on a short North American study tour. Her neighbours thoughtfully informed their postman that they thought she'd left the country, and so, with no legitimate instructions, he stopped delivering her mail. In fact he began returning it to her friends and family around the world, causing much confusion and distress.

Once I mailed two identically addressed envelopes to a friend who had spent over 25 years at the same address. One was delivered and the other came back marked "undeliverable."

More recently I sent one to the same person and it also was returned. This time I was angry enough to strike out the "undeliverable" and I also blacked out my return address and replaced it with the addressee's own address, and threw it back in the mailbox. He got it the next day.

Now, I have been watching the list of "undelivered mail" every time it is published, and I know that none of mine has ever been listed.

You cannot even rely on that list for accuracy.

We pay enough for this service — approximately double the charge in other countries, both for local and air mail — and we deserve something better. It is in the interest of Japanese business to demand quality postal delivery.

Part of the problem may be low morale among postal workers, but part of it is also a poor choice of postal code systems. Japan modeled its postal system on the British system, complete with the red mail boxes, but went in an inefficient way when it came to choosing a postal code system.

By switching to the American model, Japan has ended up with postal code districts as large as half a ward.

If Japan had followed either the British or Canadian systems, we would have postal code areas so specific that you could tell from the code not only in which city block it was located, but on which of the four sides of the block.

Many years ago I received a letter from another country addressed simply: Joan

Kabayama, Canada K2G 0W2. My postal code applies to only 34 houses and our postal carrier knew all of them very well. By using a combination of hiragana and digits, instead of the Roman alphabet and digits, it would be possible to identify even smaller areas very conveniently, by postal code alone.

I strongly recommend that the Japanese postal code system be completely reorganized, especially if automated machine-sorting is seriously being considered.

Getting to know the postman is important!

Uncommon
sense

Have you ever had a conversation with someone in which you were both using the same vocabulary and yet the conversation did not make "sense?"

Did you feel as if you were each firing your words over the other person's shoulder, just missing him?

For a long time I have had this uneasy feeling when talking even with very fluent Japanese speakers of English, every time the expression "common sense" was involved.

In English, "common sense" means innate intelligence, or natural ability, as for example in the case where the head of a small business must be absent and cannot be contacted, and says to his secretary, "If there are any decisions which must be made in my absence, please go ahead and use your own good judgement." The closest in meaning in Japanese is *ryoshiki*.

I find that what most Japanese are translating into English as "common sense" is *jyoshiki* which is really the closest equivalent of the English "public opinion."

Since we've often seen public opinions formed based upon misinformation, or half-truths, this helps to explain the confusion when public opinion is translated as "common sense." Perhaps this is the result of translating the words "common" and "sense" separately, rather than as a complete expression.

I find this even more confusing than the use of borrowed words where the meaning is changed, such as *arubaito*, which comes from *arbeit* meaning "work" in German, but is adopted as "part-time work" in Japanese, or even when the meaning is turned almost opposite such as *feminisuto* a distortion of the English word "feminist" — some one who supports equal rights for women in the legal and economic spheres, and in Japan refers to a man who holds doors open for women, or holds the chair for women to be seated!

What they really mean

There are a few humorous phrases that crop up regularly in reports of traffic accidents in Japan.

The first and most common is that the victim received "injuries, requiring, for example, three month-treatment."

Now the accident may just have happened yesterday! How on Earth could anyone guess in advance, how long recovery would take?

First I asked a newspaperman, who said it was in the police reports. Next, I asked a police friend, and he said they got it from the doctor who examined the victim upon arrival in hospital.

The young daughter of another newspaperman was victim of such a car accident last year.

The attending doctor made exactly such a pronouncement — injuries requiring three months' treatment" — but the young lady recovered in a week and left the hospital.

"We always tend to overestimate," a doctor told me, "because if it takes longer than we predict, the patient will think we are incompetent."

It seems, too, that the public likes to have these estimates as a way of judging the seriousness of an accident, whereas in other countries we would only say that the person was slightly injured, seriously injured, or critically injured.

If an estimate of recovery time were given, it would be acknowledged to be an estimate.

The other frequently-used peculiar expression is that the driver was charged with "professional negligence" causing injury of death. This is a direct translation of the Japanese expression *gyomujo*.

However, you may go on to read that the driver was a student or a housewife. Rarely was the driver a taxi driver, or a truck driver, or someone's chauffeur. Sometimes the person is even unemployed, so there is no way it could be his "profession."

If your surgeon left his scissors inside you, you could charge him with *gyomujo*. Or, if a machine-operator (whose job it was) caused an accident and injured a person or property, that person could be charged with *gyomujo*.

I was recently asked if I could ever be

charged with "professional negligence" if I caused an accident in Canada. "No," I replied, "even if I were carrying a station wagon load of students to an athletic competition and caused an accident in which they were injured, although the parents of the children might later sue me, the police could never make such a charge."

Law-abiding foreigners

Some of my Japanese friends were surprised, after reading the screaming headlines, when they discovered that the National Police Agency annual report for 1987 showed how much more law-abiding foreign residents there are than even the average law-abiding Japanese.

The figures show that although foreigners are only one percent of the population, they are actually responsible for less than one-fifth of one percent of crime.

By contrast, perhaps because they are so trusting, or because they are thought to be carrying more cash (a false assumption, actually), they are more than ten times as likely to be the victims of crime.

My friends asked me whether such a display of honesty was a reflection of the foreigners' religious background, to make such significant difference in trustworthiness.

I believe the answer lies in another direction. In the same report it states that well over 50 percent of violent crimes are committed by unemployed Japanese youth. The difference is not religious, ethnic or cultural: it is economic.

There are almost no unemployed foreigners in Japan. Most are here on working visas, and if they lose their jobs they must leave. People with a reasonably good job are unlikely to commit crimes. They also know the risks of deportation.

The number of foreign young people here on their own is also not that great, certainly not as many as the international agreements regarding "working holiday" visitors had anticipated.

Nations wishing to reduce their crime rate must do two things. The first is to adopt and enforce strict gun-control laws. In Japan, if firearms are stolen, the whole area of the city is cordoned off and police conduct a house to house search until they are found.

The second is to show more concern about the employment of young people, especially school drop-outs. In Western countries the unemployment rate among young people is double the national average. Young people need a sense of self-worth and an outlet for their energies.

A law-abiding myth

In September 1987, in the Washington Post, a writer alleged that it is respect for the law that keeps crime low in Japan. For a couple of years I have been exploring what I now feel is just another Instant Expert Myth. I find that I am not alone in being suspicious of that hypothesis.

In the *Daily Yomiuri* editorial of October 19,1987, dealing with flagrant abuses of copyright and widespread piracy of videotaped U.S. films, the following statement appeared: "It is important to formulate a system of law, but more important to drive home the spirit of respecting copyrights among the people." It is safe to conclude that most Japanese do not appear to respect copy right law.

Takashi Shinozaki, University of Tokyo law student, in his prize-winning essay in the U.S.-Japan Student Essay Contest in February 1988 made this observation: "A recent survey showed that Japanese feel that laws are *some-*

thing to be operated with some adaptation to circumstances .... or something to be adopted with flexibility or sometimes to be neglected." He felt that this showed that Japanese respect (economic) reality such as profits, rather than laws which are more like principles. In other words, his observations reflected my own on the subject of contracts.

We have seen many other examples of flouting of the law, including the operations of Yakuza gangs, wide-spread tax evasion, and bribery. Illegal corporal punishment and cruelty inflicted by teachers in schools, goes largely unpunished.

A writer in the *Japan Times* (October 28,1987) finds it rather hard "to find a highly developed sense of law here." What may be mistaken for "respect for the law," Kevin Gregg identifies as "a disturbingly strong respect for authority ... at whatever cost to law and justice."

Fear itself may be a significant factor. We have surely read many cases where convictions have been made, based on forced confessions alone, to be aware of this element of fear.

An interesting point was made in the November 1987 issue of *PHP Intersect* magazine, suggesting that the fact that so much crime goes unreported, is due to the intimidating tactics by some police toward the victims of crime. This would help explain why cases of rape, for example, go largely unreported. This makes Japanese crime statistics very unreliable.

Considering the fact that the Anti-Prostitution Law, was enacted in 1956, and so little effort appears to be made to enforce it, it would seem that if a profit can be made by influential, albeit undesirable members of this society, then law and justice become insignificant.

Having been narrowly missed on several occasions by drivers trying to "beat the traffic light" at my corner, right in front of the police station next to Kodansha, my impression of Japanese drivers is not that of respect for the law.

In the summer of 1987 I conducted my own small survey among the senior sociology class at Sophia University. I asked if they were very conscious of the law and very careful to obey it in general.

Their reaction was to say that they did not think much about the law, and, if they did, it was to feel that the law had nothing to do with them.

A friend of mine who is a police detective

in the field of computer crime, a typically "white collar" crime, does not view his fellow-citizens as very respectful of the law.

What is this phenomenon that has been so widely mistaken for "respect for the law?"

The element of "being seen" is very strong. It seems that tax evasion, or most "white collar" crime that is almost invisible, or the illegal taping done in the privacy of one's home, seem to be accompanied by almost no sense of guilt.

Not only is it necessary "not to be seen," but "not being seen by someone we know" seems to play an important role. While visiting some other countries there are Japanese who commit crimes against women and children which they would not normally commit in their own community.

Clearly, what appears to others as "respect for the law" among Japanese is a mistaken ethnocentric observation.

Special sports center

During the winter vacation I had the pleasure of visiting the Tokyo Municipal Sports Center for the Handicapped in Kita-ku.

There, a medical referral is necessary in order to enjoy the facilities, except for the companion or attendant accompanying a handicapped person. A medical is also given on the first visit, and one's blood pressure is checked each subsequent visit.

The modern, easily accessible building features a basketball court of nearly 750 square meters and a beautiful six-lane, 25 meter pool. The day I was there the sun was shining in across the surface of the water, which was at comfortably warm temperature ideal for arthritis and other disabilities.

To reach this complex we took the west exit from the Yurakucho Line at Ikebukuro Station, where a small bus operates, free of charge, every hour on the hour.

It takes about half an hour to reach the sports center.

If it is swimming you are interested in, you may go in on the hour, until 10 minutes before the next hour.

There is an attractive, licensed coffee shop for light meals, and a recreational lounge with a TV. The bus leaves on the half hour for the return trip to Ikebukuro Station.

This is a splendid facility, particularly for the nonworking handicapped. My only regret was that the time required made it difficult for the working handicapped to take full advantage.

For example: to enjoy a 50-minute swim there was the half-hour wait before and after, because of the bus schedule, and the half-hour bus ride each way. That meant, about three hours plus the time from home or work to Ikebukuro, in order to enjoy a 50-minute swim.

I wish that more attention could be given to providing recreation opportunities in many parts of the city, together with non-disabled members of the public.

Curling in Japan

A few weeks ago I had my first experience to see live curling. It does sound a little ridiculous, doesn't it, to come to Japan to see curling? The occasion was the Canada Cup competition, televised by CBC. (You may have seen me among the crowd.)

The Canada Cup is a trophy given in Japan, and was won a year ago by a team of local Canadians in Tokyo, even though Canada sent a team.

This year Canada sent its world champion women's team which won of course, with some embarrassingly one-sided scores, like 13-1 and 9-0. However, we think that in another year Japan will have several outstanding teams, as this sport really seems to have caught on.

Teams of any kind in Japan always appear in attractive uniforms, as their curling teams did, in fact, this year's women's team appeared attired in short Tartan skirts and tights. The local Canadian team, in contrast presented a rather informal, motley appearance but the play was good.

To our surprise, our team won over some 17 teams in its division and won a set of team sweaters.

The teams were ceremoniously piped in by a fully-kilted and decked out bagpipe band, and when they got up close we could see that they were entirely Japanese pipers. They certainly knew what they were doing, and were very well received by the crowd.

After such a high-class introduction to this sport, I shall certainly go out to watch again.

Not a homestay
after all

A few years ago my family had a very expensive, unfortunate experience, which resulted from a cultural misunderstanding.

A Japanese scientist whom we had met here in Tokyo at an international conference was transferred to Chicago, with his wife and children. they sent us a photo of their new suburban home, and urged us repeatedly to visit them in Chicago. Finally we agreed to make the trip, along with two of our children. We also took a very fine ornamental platter which was a little beyond our budget in those days as a house gift to our hosts.

When we arrived we presented our acquaintances with the gift, and were taken on a guided tour of their new home. We were downstairs in the basement "family room," a comfortable large room, with its own bathroom, when we asked where we should put our suitcases. The father of the family said,

"Oh, I've reserved a motel room for you, not far from here." We protested that we would be quite alright downstairs, and actually we did not want to put him to any expense, but he said that it was already reserved.

In North America, families, and many people who travel by car, stay in motels rather than in hotels, because there is no charge for parking, and the car is usually parked just outside your unit, very conveniently.

The motel room was quite roomy with two double beds for the four of us, but our family was not used to being confined in one room, and after two or three days the excess of "togetherness" was beginning to take its toll, and showed up in frayed tempers. At one point I was afraid that one of us might be killed in a fit of anger.

We also soon realized that we were intended to pay for the motel room ourselves, an expense which we had not counted on.

The problem was that we had assumed that a "homestay" was part of the invitation, when it was not. In our cultural background when we invite someone to visit us we expect to provide the hospitality. Our acquaintances hadn't been in Chicago long enough to make that adjustment.

Some of my Japanese friends complain that

I go over plans with them in too much detail. Actually what I am trying to do is to avoid some such embarrassing or uncomfortable situations from happening. Even if two people speak the same language, misunderstandings can take place, so how much greater the risk is if one of them is using a second language!

Good language move?

I was really very impressed when I first read about the Tokyo metropolitan government office of education's ambitious new English education plan. Beginning next April, all 1,900 first-year high school classes will have one hour per week of their regular English classes with a native speaker.

Based on the experience of New York State over 25 years ago, twice the benefit would be obtained if this program were offered at the middle school level rather than in the senior high school.

Educational aspects aside, there remain very serious obstacles to the ability of the Tokyo Board of Education to attract and retain good foreign teachers.

These obstacles lie in the board's own hiring policies, which they have shown no sign of changing.

First, unlike many other school boards, this board limits foreign teachers to 200 hours of teaching per year. This wipes out any possibility of experience and continuity.

Pay is per class hour taught - nothing for preparation, teachers' meetings or informal interaction with students, no vacation pay, and no *teiki* or transportation allowance.

Finally, only residents of Tokyo can be hired. Perhaps this kind of loyalty can be demanded of full-time employees. I know, for example, that in North America public school boards take rather a dim view of employees who choose to send their own children to private schools. This is similar.

However, realistically, have you tried recently to rent accommodation in Tokyo with only a part-time job? Or even two part-time jobs? A major revision of working conditions is required before I will be convinced that the board really wants quality language instruction.

Moral education,
is it?

You may remember the Ministry of Education's pronouncement very late in 1987, that "moral education" would be emphasized in the final decade of this century. For the past two years I have been part of a group of Japanese professionals meeting once a week to discuss topics of common concern.

One evening we hose the ministry's new proposals for grades one to six as our discussion topic. First, there is the problem which may not be obvious to some people, in translating "moral." In English speaking countries "moral education" means developing the ability and skills to make ethical choices and decisions throughout one's life at increasing levels of difficulty.

In Japanese, however, it becomes clear that what is referred to as "moral education" would be more correctly translated as developing "socially acceptable" behaviour. Looked at from this perspective, you can see that it is possible for something to be "socially acceptable" by one definition and yet also be "immoral" by another definition.

For example, we need only look at grades one and two where the curriculum objective is to "teach discipline." If by that, "self-discipline" is meant, then the Japanese language and the English-language definition are congruent. However, if the Japanese is interpreted as "developing fear of authority," then our definitions are in fact mutually exclusive.

We looked at the objectives for grades three and four, to "love the nation." One of my friends, a university professor with two elementary school children, said, "This is impossible. Love of nation, like love of family cannot be taught. It is something that happens naturally. That is, it develops on its own."

I was glad that it was a well-educated thoughtful Japanese person who made that observation. While I had been thinking the same thoughts, I had not expressed them, for fear of distorting the discussion with my own cultural bias. We went on to look at the aims for grades five and six, "to learn respect of Japanese culture," and we wish to make the following proposal.

The study of Japanese culture, and the development of admiration and respect for it, should be lowered to grades three and four. "Love of nation" will be an automatic out-growth of this cultural study. It will happen on its own.

In the two years saved, grades five and six, we suggest a new program: "respect for other cultures." This would fill a large gap in the preparation of Japanese children, and would come at a stage where they usually also study the geography of other lands.

There are two obvious defects in the way the Ministry of Education forms its commit-tees to recommend changes in the education system. In selecting a "committee of wise men," there seems to be no effort to select educators from all levels, or even to include parents. Until the Monbusho ensures such knowledgeable participation, we will continue to receive unrealistic, unworkable recommen-dation and teachers will be blamed for not im-plementing the unimplementable!

Even good recommendation can be sabo-taged if educators do not feel a responsibility and commitment to them. Isn't it too bad that the Ministry of Education fails to take advan-tage of one of the basic tenets of Japanese business, that of group decision-making and consensus-building?

Intelligence
tests

Not only is it hard to find intelligence tests that are "culture fair," that is, not biased in favour of middle-and upper-class children familiar with musical instruments and other cultural vocabulary, but we have another, totally unrecognized problem.

Some of the things we teach "as fact" in one society are so totally unacceptable in another that a student who gives the "right answer" from his home culture, might be regarded as lacking in intelligence if he gave the same answer in another culture.

A few examples come immediately to mind. When I took my first grade reading course for elementary school children in Japan, one of the experiences we did was to identify opposites. This sounds easy. The opposite of *big* is *small,* and the opposite of *up* is *down,* and *inside* is the opposite of *outside.* But what is the opposite of *white*?

The commonly accepted opposite of *white*

is *black*. That is, the full colour spectrum as opposed to a complete absence of light.

Such is not the case in a first grade Japanese text book, where we find the expected answer is *red*. This may surprise you until you remember that Japan has a red and white flag, and red is the "other" colour.

In team sports you will also see a red team and a white team. However, Canada also has a red and white flag, but no Canadian school child is taught that red and white are opposites.

To find the opposite of *red*, we turn to one of the sciences either physics or biology - to find that red and green are complementary colours, both from the colour spectrum and the physiological structure of the eye, itself.

Another interesting pair of opposites found in this first grade Japanese textbook is *male* and *female*.

I have always been taught that sexual characteristics form a continuum from extremely feminine at one end to extremely masculine at the other, with the largest numbers of people constituting two "modes," or two areas of greatest frequency along that continuum.

As a mathematician I would refer to it as a *bimodal distribution* of characteristics. This point of view was supported by an international medical conference only last year, in which the position was taken that males and females are 95 percent the same and only five percent different in structure.

It should follow then that similarities, rather than differences, should be stressed.

Isn't it interesting that people in one society grow up accepting as fact some things which make no sense in another society?

You can see why some "opinions" are, unfortunately, thought of as "not very intelligent."

Teaching discourtesy

One recent Friday afternoon I had a frightening experience. I was on the Seibu-Ikebukuro line, with my younger son, on the way to spend the weekend with our best friends in Saitama-ken. The train was crowded with excited young people as schools had just been dismissed for the day.

A middle-aged man, who was with an older woman, took a look at my grey hair and my slight physical handicap and got up, giving me his seat. Within 15 minutes or so his body was sagging as he hung on to the swaying straps. He appeared to have fainted, still standing, but I feared he was having a heart attack. My son, who was standing in front of me, helped me to ease him back into the seat which he had given up for me.

No one got up to make room for him to lie down. His mother, who was with him, said he had just been working too many hours lately, when we expressed our concern. I thought about the fact that in Britain, children's and students' reduced fares are clearly marked, "for standees." When I see children here dashing past adults into the subway cars to occupy seats before the older persons who are paying full-fare, or I see those parents who allow, or even encourage, their children to remain seated while older people are standing, I feel that many children in Japan are learning bad habits.

Unfortunately, the courteous young people are not as conspicuous as the thoughtless ones. Japanese adults tell me that they are also distressed with the thoughtless behaviour we often see in subways and trains, but are too embarrassed to speak to other people's children.

If it is too much to expect of today's parents, to educate children in matters of public courtesy, perhaps it is not too much to ask the metropolitan subway system to advertise widely that reduced fares are for standing room and that preschool children may travel free "when not occupying a seat."

Courtesy is habit-forming, but it is a habit which must be formed early.

Not meaning
to be rude

On a recent visit I was invited to an international elementary school in Yokosuka, and was seated in a Grade Three class, answering questions about Canada.

One small boy raised his hand, smiled, and asked, "Please, how old are you?" His teacher was obviously uncomfortable and was about to reprimand him, before I interrupted her. "It's quite alright," I said, turning to the boy. "That's a good question, but you see I don't feel that I know you well enough to answer that one." He seemed satisfied, and turned to another subject.

I knew, of course, that one's age in Japan is **not** considered personal information. I remember during my first visit to Japan, when swimming in a public pool, a youngster came paddling up to me asking, "How old are you, lady?" The child's teacher was quite relieved that I had not made a big issue of this cultural difference, and did not embarrass the child.

Katakannibalization of the Japanese language

A recent letter-to-the-editor in one of the Tokyo English language newspapers, has prompted me to share my feelings on this topic.

Ms. Yoshiko Morita, from Iruma, wrote to protest the infiltration of the Japanese language by unnecessary Katakana.

Not only are the pronunciations distorted, so are the meanings, often ending up opposite to the original words upon which they were modelled. (*Feminisuto* comes to my mind, as a good example.)

Often, as Ms. Morita discovered, they are completely "made-up" words which cannot be found in a dictionary because they are not found in **any** lanuage

Katakana is not only a problem for Japanese.

It presents the same guessing game to foreigners, too.

When my mother and father-in-law retired and returned to Japan after nearly 40 years in Canada, they found the Japanese language greatly changed, but the **worst** part was the KATAKANA, which seems to have invaded the language like a virus.

With my background, having been raised in Quebec, (the French-speaking province of Canada), where the Ministry of Education is very strict in its opposition to "loan words", you can understand how I resent the use of this Katakana vocabulary, **where there are perfectly** good Japanese words for the same thing.

One day I puzzled over an ad on the subway. I was really angry to see a one-syllable English word "gold" twisted into a three-syllable monstrosity — *goh-roo-doh* — when there is a perfectly good Japanese word — *kin*.

The media are mostly at fault because these are used extensively in advertising to catch the reader's attention. What good does it do, when having caught your attention, the **meaning escapes?**

Worst still, these Katakannibalized expressions interfere with the correct pronunciation when people try to learn a second language. It's like learning the dog-paddle on your own, rather than taking swimming lessons and having bad habits to unlearn if you later wish to become a competitive swimmer!

Did you know that the small nation of Iceland does not permit **any** loan words to be used?

Certainly the government publications should take the lead in avoiding Katakana, and the advertising media must accept their responsibility in preserving Japanese Language and culture.

More on Japanese handwriting

The thought struck me while observing others, and exploring my own experience with the Japanese writing system, how much easier life should be here in Japan for left-handed people! Japanese being written from top to bottom, starting at the upper right-hand corner of the page, means that left-handed persons have the advantage of not dragging their hand over their writing and smudging. Japanese script consists of some 50 phonetic symbols for Japanese words, and some 50 more phonetic symbols used for foreign or "borrowed" words, which supplement and connect the thousands of Kanji or ideographs which make up the language.

I have discussed my observations with Japanese teachers who agree with my conclusions. We therefore find it ironic, and totally unacceptable,that here in this land of contrasts there are still teachers who punish their left-handed pupils for writing with their left-hand!

Teaching disrespect for books

This morning, on my way home from the Post Office and grocery store, I passed a private home where the garbage was out for collection. Beside it, neatly tied up in three piles, were forty to fifty soft and hard covered books in good condition.

Just a few doors down, and across the narrow street is a second hand book shop where you can get such used books for about Y150, or $1.50 Cdn, yet the house-holder did not even think about donating those books to this neighbour.

Every March, at the end of the Japanese academic year, garbage bins, especially outside apartment buildings, are filled to overflowing with text books. While I can understand that Japanese homes are so small that, with few exceptions, there is no place to store such things, the vast amount of garbaging of books, in a country where new books cost an arm and a leg, is a serious matter.

The fault lies, I believe with the school system. In its attempt to provide equal educational opportunity to all children up to the end of Grade Nine, or through junior high school, the Japanese school system gives each child a free set of books every year.

A large proportion of the school budget is spent on books in Japan, much higher than in Canada, where Canadian book publishers complain, with considerable justification, that Canadian School Boards are rather cheap when it comes to purchasing books. In Canada we loan them to our students, expect them to be well cared for, and be used by from four to six students.

Here I see the Japanese attitude in my college, where students scribble on their texts, (most of which have been brought in from outside the country) as they think of them as being disposable. This was shocking to me coming from an environment in which to write in a text book was just one short step away from blasphemy.

Soft-covered books and comic books, bought to while away the tedious hours on the subway, are later abandoned on the subway.

Canadian school children would trade such

comics with their friends until the covers fell off.

I am certain that such an attitude was never foreseen or anticipated by the Japanese educational establishment! This is a good example of the fact that we often fail to teach what we think we are teaching, and end up teaching something quite different.

The Education Ministry Monbusho is considering stopping the provision of free texts altogether as an economic measure. Considering the cost of textbooks I feel this would place an unfair burden on those families who can least afford it.

I strongly urge the ministry to first consider a system of textbook loan or rental.

Of course the biggest objections will come from the publishers of school textbooks. Let us hope that the ministry will place the needs of the students ahead of the wishes of private enterprise in this case.

University entrance exams

There are several problems which must be addressed. The first is the question of what is being measured by these examinations and whether what is being measured is actually of any value in university.

Second, is the matter of what the existence of these examinations does to the whole secondary school system.

Thirdly, since a university may be the best in one field of study, while another is better in a second area of study, and so on, how can we help the student and his or her parents to decide which is the "best university" for that student?

First, in acknowledging the fact that entrance examinations measure only short-term memory, and do not measure understanding, or the ability to use the knowledge one has, means that we must question whether these examinations have **any** value in selecting students for university.

My own college students admitted that a few months after the school year had begun they had forgotten so much that they could no longer have passed the entrance exam!

The pressure to pass exams has reached the point where a junior high history teacher told me that if a student really likes history and asks a question, not only the teacher but his or her classmates are likely to say, "Don't ask questions or we won't have time to finish the course."

I feel that the examination system has totally distorted the high school programme, and, in many ways the "unfitted" the student for university level study.

Too little thought is given to matching the student with the most appropriate programme. A 25-year old man told me he wished he had known more about what he wanted to do in life when he went to university, because he felt that his years at university were largely wasted.

Since only about 35 to 40 per cent of Japanese attend any university, never mind a "famous" university, it is obviously not essential for a happy and fulfilling life.

It is important to work for a better balance of numbers between male and female students in university.

Even with the 1986 Equal Employment Opportunity Law, if there are four times as many males graduating as females, the young women are still unlikely to get the most challenging jobs.

Since Japanese universities, with the notable exception of Kyoto University, do not have a good record in producing Nobel Prize Winners, (one measure of academic excellence) we might also ask our universities to redefine their purposes, and judge how well they are accomplishing these aims.

Words and
attitudes

In what ways do the media reflect social attitudes and to what extent do they shape them? And does our language serve to express our thinking, or does it in some ways limit or distort our thinking? My own interest in these questions was stimulated at a recent meeting of the Society of Writers, Editors and Translators.

The topic was *Non-biased Communication. Avoiding Sexist Language in the Media.* The panel speakers were New York Times correspondent Susan Chira, AP Asian news editor James Smith, EDS Inc. editor and translator Suzanne Trumbull and Kazue Suzuki of Asahi News.

Reference was made to the style guides of The New York Times and The Associated Press, which differ slightly. By comparison it was interesting to note that the Asahi and Kyodo News Service guidebooks cover the topics of how to refer acceptably to handicapped persons and racial groups but devote no space to sex-discriminatory language.

The first government body in Japan to adopt an impartial language policy is Kanagawa-ken.

It was very interesting to examine what has happened as a result of press codes in the treatment of racial groups and the handicapped. Since I was living in the United States in the late '50s and during the '60s, I was very sensitive to racial epithets. Now we don't see them in the media, and they have generally fallen into disuse. We now avoid using racially insulting terms, because they offend people.

Here the press code now precludes crude remarks about the handicapped. To a large extent, I believe this responsible behaviour on the part of the media has resulted in a change in public attitudes toward the handicapped, and we are beginning to see more social participation by such groups.

We need to apply the same standards when writing about women. Curiously, Kyodo News Service does not yet accept the term "spouse" as the correct word for husband or wife, although for at least 30 years it has been the term used in the U.S. Immigration Act and related documents.

Japanese, as a language, is relatively gender-free. The problem is with underlying attitudes. You may read 20 pages of a book, according to one of the panellists, and only discover on page 21 that the writer has used "people" to mean males only, because on page 21 the writer has the "people" going home to their wives!

Commenting on the fact that as recently as 1986, only 6.4 percent of all Japanese media employees were women, a Japanese member of the audience said that he felt we needed more women in the newsroom, to provide a better balance and perspective.

He also urged those of us in the English-language press to continue reporting vigorously about the problems of Japanese minorities. He feels that we are being read by the Japanese public and are having a positive effect on this society.

As a society, however, we still tolerate sexist pejoratives which we now would not allow if directed at a racial group. Seeing and hearing these words leads us to think in those terms.

Most of the terms in Japanese for "wife" are pejorative, but because they are heard so often, what is "common" has become "natural". Sexism is very subtle and can be almost subliminal. So much so that an otherwise intelligent and sensitive Japanese man not long ago flatly denied that Japan is a sexist society!

We must realize that writing style changes do lead to changes in attitude. When I was a child, half a century ago, I recall hearing a woman exclaim, "But we treated him white!" She was totally unaware that this was a racist remark.

I also recall hearing a man shout in anger to a French-Canadian, "Speak white!" If we can raise our children without these racist and sexist epithets to use in anger or in thoughtlessness, we will have taken a major step toward a better society.

So much for
so little

Ed Koch, mayor of New York City, in his call for a citizen's boycott of movie houses in his city, refers to the recent price increase as "an outrage."

Ticket prices there have risen from $5 to $6 and then $7 (almost Y1,000). I agree than this is an outrageous price for a movie. Visitors and resident foreigners, coming from major North American cities, where we are accustomed to paying the equivalent of Y500 in Canada and perhaps Y600 or Y700 in the United States, not to mention our regular "half-price Tuesdays," are amazed that Tokyo residents do not riot when charged Y1,500 to see the same films.

Part of the answer is that it is not in the Japanese character to riot or even protest when they are overcharged from double (such as air fares or long distance calls) to ten times as much as other people are paying (as in the case of beef or rice).

Another part of the answer is that, with only six or seven percent of the Japanese public travelling abroad every year, most do not know the extent to which they are being exploited. They have been told they have a very high standard of living and have come to believe it.

A third factor, which applies to most forms of entertainment and at least half of overseas travel, is that so much of it is paid for as business expenses. Why riot or even question the price if someone else is paying?

Unfortunately the ordinary family suffers in being unable to afford to go to the theatre or to restaurants or on vacation together.

There is also a conspiracy on the part of the travel industry, to prevent Japanese from learning about cheaper travel costs elsewhere. Recently a Canadian who came here two years ago was refused a one-way ticket to Canada by Japan Air Lines. "We do not sell one-way tickets," was the firm position taken by JAL. Most Japanese would not think of checking out another airline.

I feel very badly when I see my Japanese friends working so hard and getting so little in return.

Inflatable
accessories

One morning I walked into my college classroom and saw, to my puzzled amusement, that the three young ladies at the first table seemed to share the same set of initials. They all had their purses or handbags on the desk, all of different sizes, from a little one with a thin shoulder strap to a large one almost big enough to be an overnight bag.

The thing that aroused my curiosity was that the material, colour and pattern of each was identical, and they were covered with the same initials! I asked whether the girls were sisters, since I know a family in which the three sons are named David, Derek and Douglas. Their father's name is Donald, and there's quite some confusion with the mail, most of which is addressed to "D. Hanson."

My students then explained that the initials on the bags were those of the designer. Since then I have tried to be more observant about what people are carrying on the subways. I've even seen a man carrying a briefcase covered with the same patterned, initialled plastic.

More surprising is the fact that these items are not cheap. I spotted an ad in a Canadian newspaper in which some of them were shown at prices ranging up to the equivalent of Y75,000. Knowing the Japanese distribution system, I would wager the price is about double in Tokyo. At a recent international social gathering here, this bag phenomenon came up for discussion.

A Canadian man asked, "They're very well made. Why wouldn't you consider buying one?"

"Because they're **plastic**," I replied. "And they all look alike," added my friend the lawyer, a lady from Brazil.

Soon after that, I visited Canada, and was amazed to discover among the junk-mail inserts in my Saturday newspaper an ad for one of those name-brand bags. A famous label carry-all was available for the equivalent of only Y700 (that's seven hundred yen!) plus a "proof-of-purchase" for a certain brand of coffee-something available for another Y300 or so (about $3.00)

I was tempted to buy 10 of them and bring them back to Japan as *omiyage*, and give away the coffee.

What
aid?

In recent months we have read repeated criticisms of Japan's (and other nations') foreign aid.

To begin with, some industrial nations give much more generously than others. Norway and Holland (the latter with a higher population density, incidentally, than Japan) gave three or four times the percentage of their gross national product as did the United States and Japan in 1986. So some nations are much more conscious of their international responsibilities, or their society responds better to the needs of others.

Quantity is not the only dimension of the problem.

Many nations offer almost exclusively "tied aid," that is, schemes in which a grant is made on condition that over 70 percent of the money is spent in the donor country, even if needs could be met at less cost elsewhere.

Or we have matching grants, whereby the

recipient country must put up an equal sum of money to finance a project chosen by the donor country.

Often the bulk of so-called aid is taken up by "administration costs" in the form of salaries for "advisers" from the donor nation.

The worst "aid" comes as loans. Even if interest rates are low, and Japanese interest rates may be only half U.S. rates, the interest owed on foreign debt by some of the poorest countries amount to half their GNP. Thus we have the phenomenon that over 20 percent of Japan's designated ODA in recent years is not taken up. Some countries are so poor they cannot afford our aid.

How dare we label as "aid" any program in which as little as 15-30 percent of the total actually reaches the needy? Yet this is exactly what happens when the adminstration of charitable donations is handled by private business. Even a gift from one government to another is subject to the same defects.

We, in the donor countries, have great trust in our governments, which by and large are quite stable, but we fail to recognize that many third world countries do not have stable governments, and we fail to anticipate a high degree of misappropriation of such gifts.

In the case of food aid, for example, much

of it ends up in the stomachs of the military, who are already among the best fed in countries with rampant malnutrition.

One of the best proposals I have heard is that Japanese businesses set up a revolving no-interest loan fund, to help establish small businesses in third-world countries. While the fund could be added to, every year, its chief virtue lies in aiding individuals to become self-sufficient and able to repay the loans, so that others may be helped.

A second proposal is that Japanese scientists and businessmen be encouraged, following their normal retirement, to serve as volunteer advisers in developing countries. One Canadian couple I know who did something like this came back from Botswana after a five-year stint looking 10 years younger. Wouldn't this be a splendid way to use the talents of some of our youthful retires?

We have two significant problems ahead of us: how to provide aid that is of genuine value to developing nations, and how to help our own senior citizens to live healthy, satisfying lives.

Being mugged
in Tokyo...

Now I can write about it, but I could not at the time. Japan has a well-deserved reputation for safety, and non-violence.

Actually the density of the population and the near absence of privacy result in a very high proportion of criminals actually being caught. Until last August I had nothing more serious stolen than a new bar of soap, on two occasions, by members of the university swim team, when I was here at summer school in 1985 — they were the only ones in the locker room at the time!

Last August, however, I was not so lucky. I had only been back here an hour from my summer vacation in Canada, when a colleague of mine invited me to dinner within two blocks of our Y residence to celebrate my return. As we left the restaurant a little after 7 p.m. someone charged into me, at a run, from behind, and took off down the block with my wallet. Half way down the block he jumped onto a bicycle, which he must have left parked there and vanished into the distance, down a street too small for a car to follow. My friend, a lady older than me, took after him bravely, but lost him when he got to his bicycle.

We called the police who came immediately and were very kind. They cruised the streets with us for about an hour. They said that although such crimes were very few, they had doubled in the past year.

What was so upsetting to me was not the loss of money, as I carry very little, but the loss of my Canadian citizenship card, my credit cards, cheque book and cheque register, and all my most important telephone numbers and addresses. My finances were thoroughly upset, and are not fully unscrambled yet.

Or course I had to make long distance calls to Canada to cancel the credit cards. I felt especially badly because the wallet itself was a brand new leather one, a gift from two of my children who could ill-afford it.

I had never had this kind of experience before, and although I don't consider myself a materialist, I took to my bed in shock for two days and lost five pounds, because I couldn't eat. None of the contents of my wallet have been found.

Honest differences

Honesty, I find, means different things in different societies. In North America, if you leave something valuable in a public place, you feel very fortunate indeed ever to see it again.

On the other hand, if someone does not tell the truth, you feel deeply distressed, and completely lose trust in that person. This has happened fairly recently in both Canada and the United States with regard to some of our politicians.

In Japan, by contrast (in spite of my unfortunate experience last August on Mejiro-dori of being mugged and relieved of wallet and identification documents), theft of possessions, including shoplifting and breaking and entering are rare, albeit, increasing crimes.

During my first summer in Tokyo, as part of a Canadian delegation to an international conference, I remember how deeply I was impressed by the experience of one of my colleagues. We had been taken on a tour of the city; my friend put her valuable camera down on a rock in a public park. She did not miss it for nearly three hours. When we went back, there it was, still sitting on the rock where she had left it!

If you have spent any time at the Port Authority Bus Terminal in New York City, you will understand how delighted we were to see her camera again.

Honesty in terms of frank expression of thought, however, is not common in Japan. Partly because Japanese people are not accustomed to being asked what they think, and so become very distressed and confused, and partly because in Japan it is considered "polite" to tell others what you think they want to hear, you will have too look rather hard to find candour.

Cheating, in school, is not regarded as wrong, intrinsically, but only if one is caught and causes embarrassment to one's family.

We must be especially careful when judging members of another society. For example, in many African societies, if you leave anything untended outside, it is assumed to be communal property for anyone to use or take.

In Alaska, because of the harsh winter, people leave their doors unlocked when they leave their homes, even for extended periods. They expect people, even complete strangers, to take refuge if necessary. The code of ethics mandates that if you use someone's home, you must leave it as clean and neat as you found it.

A common example of lack of understanding of other cultures on the part of Japanese police is their assumption that people are lying.

My fully bilingual best friend has witnessed Japanese policemen shouting, "Don't lie! Tell the truth!" at a group of frightened teenage tourists, from a predominantly Catholic country, who were in trouble.

There seemed no understanding that they were too frightened to do anything but tell the truth.

Contract
differences

Much has been said recently about the differences in negotiating styles between business representatives from different countries. Of all countries, it is said that Japan and the United States present the greatest contrast in negotiating styles.

I believe that there is another difference whose significance cannot be overemphasized. That is the matter of how we interpret a contract or similar financial agreement.

When two Japanese businesses enter into an agreement it is not a one-shot deal or temporary relationship. It can, in fact, be one that lasts for two or three generations. This is why, if some problem arises for one of the signatories they feel no hesitation in contacting the other party to request a reopening or renegotiation of their "contract."

The other company would not normally try to hold the troubled one to the agreement, since that would ruin the future relationship of the two companies. It is not in the interest of either to insist on a deal that might force the other out of business.

Western companies, on the other hand, regard their contracts with such respect, as legal documents, as if there were almost an element of sacredness about them. A European or North American company, for example, that wins a contract with a low bid, and then recognizes that it can only fulfil this contract at a loss, will still complete the contract at the agreed price. To break a contract would be regarded as dishonest, and to do so would affect the company's reputation.

In the long run, such a loss of honour could prove more costly to the company than temporary loss on one contract, which they would hope to recoup in future deals.

Let me illustrate with some recent personal experiences and observations.

I had a one-year lease on my one-room apartment, which was renewed for a second year at the same rent. Part way through the second year the management notified us of a Y3,500 per month surcharge for common facilities such as laundry room, which had formerly been entirely included in our rent. We were asked to sign a letter to say we agreed to this increase.

As I could not read the notice (written in Japanese), I refused to sign, but that did not stop the management from imposing the increase. In most countries the tenants could take their landlords to court in such circumstances. Most landlords would simply have waited until the lease renewal time, perhaps making the increase just a little higher in order to cover the higher expenses they had been experiencing.

In another case, an employer in Tokyo asked its full-time employees to return their signed contracts to exchange them for contracts at a lower rate of pay. While Japanese employees would likely have done so, the foreign employees kept photocopies of their original contract and refused to sign the new ones, even though some of them were threatened with the loss of their jobs.

The Japanese employer looked upon the employment "contract" as a flexible agreement subject to amendment, and could not understand why the foreign employees were so outraged!

This same company requested its staff to accept a postponement of their normal summer vacation to the winter of 1988, due to building remodelling, and widely advertised the changed schedule of services. Later, when they found that their construction work was ahead of schedule, they informed their employees of a new work timetable which would have had the effect of taking these employees' vacation away from them a second time. This employer was shocked when its foreign staff were prepared to take legal action against the employer for breach of contract.

Not only have we cultural differences to contend with, but we are using the same word, "contract," with two different meanings. The difference is so great that we should really not be using the same word "contract" for it.

We have yet again an illustration of the problems which arise when a word is "translated" and given quite a different meaning.

Distribution economics

Last summer a Japanese friend was on a business trip to North America. During his travels he was invited for a homestay with one of his business acquaintances, and they began talking about the cost of living.

The Japanese visitor expressed his astonishment over the fact that so many Japanese-made goods could be bought more cheaply, in some cases much more cheaply in North America. His host replied, "Some people here call it *dumping*."

Actually, while genuine cases of "dumping" undoubtedly exist, the gap is much more likely to be due to our very different methods of distribution. The warehouse price may even have been the same. The many-layered, complex Japanese dealership system causes the price to inflate with every change of hands before it gets to the customer.

The Japanese buyer pays very dearly as a result.

On the
Tokyo subway

Many people spend over an hour each way going to work in this city of twelve million people. Just think, we could put half of the population of Canada into this one City! It is not uncommon to take two or three subways or trains, or one bus and two subways.

It reminds me of my early teaching days in Montreal, when I was living in N.D.G. and teaching in Ville St. Laurent, except that in those days it was busses and street-cars I was using.

Here it takes me 45 minutes to get to the college: about 15 minutes walk from my residence to the subway station, down a narrow street that can only be partly accessed by car. Depending on the time of day, the subways run a minute to a few minutes apart.

It is only a seven-minute ride to the third stop, where I transfer to a J.N.R. train. After a few minutes going from one station to the ad-

joining station I have another seven-minute ride, again to the third station, where I have about a seven-minute walk to the college. The total, door-to-door takes me almost 45 minutes.

While I have a normal teaching load, it is spread over various mornings, afternoons and evenings, and as a result, I have only to battle the morning rush hour on Tuesday, Thursday and Friday.

Although I have seen white-gloved employees of the subway system which some people describe as "pushers", I have yet to see them push anyone. Rather they signal to the subway operator when it is safe to shut the doors. I suppose if part of my anatomy were sticking out of the doorway, I might appreciate a push.

Although we are packed like sardines until at least the next station, subways are a great way to meet people. Take last week as an example. One morning, the lady sitting beside me started the conversation by asking me if I spoke English. She is a pediatrician from China, studying children's lung diseases!

Another day a young man read my Operation Dismantle button that I wear on my jacket...and asked me where I was from. It turns out that he is a member of Japan's national swim team and had spent a month with a well known team in California, as a guest in a private home.

He told me the Japanese name for waterpolo, *suikyu*, and we had a great conversation. Another morning a lady moved over a bit to make room for me to sit down, and it turned out that she works in a medical clinic.

Finally, an older gentleman began talking with me, and when we found we had time to spare before work, he got off at my stop and had coffee to continue our conversation. It turned out that he owned a small noodle restaurant, and today, one of my teaching colleagues and I are going there for dinner.

Whatever you might say about this vast city, it is never dull.

Because people spend so much time travelling, for example several of my students and a few teachers spend an hour each way, they usually read or "cat-nap" (my students biggest complaint with their life, by the way, is lack of sleep). At first, I thought that perhaps people on subways were closing their eyes, for the sake of privacy, or because they didn't want to see older people or pregnant women standing in front of them and feel obliged to give up their seats. "Not at all", said a friend of mine, "they're sleeping!".

In a Japanese bar

The night before I left Japan for my summer vacation, one of my adult classes held a dinner party for me in a cafe near the college. There were more women than men in our party, but no other women in the cafe, except the waitress.

North Americans looking into most Japanese bars would think they were in a "gay" bar, because of the scarcity of female patrons. Most of the clients are colleagues socializing after work, according to the Japanese customs in which working as late as the boss, or accompanying him to the bar is almost unavoidable. It looks strange to us, being accustomed to social groups of more or less equal numbers of males and females.

This custom does, however, make Japan a more comfortable place for homosexuals. They can "date" freely without feeling conspicuous. Classical psychologists regarded homo-sexuality as a stage of life through which all males and females pass, usually in the early teens. Until fairly recently it was also held that those who maintained this homosexual preference were somehow arrested in their development and needed "treatment".

Current thinking recognizes that as far as we can determine there has always been a certain percentage of the population for whom same-sex attachments appear to be their normal orientation. It is also recognized however, that in extraordinary circumstances such as the military, or in prisons, or in segregated schools, when the opposite sex is not present, such attachments increase significantly.

In Japan, as in Canada, during the early teen-years a time when very close friendships are being established, there also seems to be an aversion, even a fear of the opposite sex occurring. Even in mixed school situations boys and girls commonly experience shyness and some embarrassment speaking to each other. In the case of girls, in both countries some parents may deliberately foster such fears. Boys, whose social skills develop somewhat later, are often the butt of jokes, because of their lack of self-confidence.

In Japan in particular, unless we are fortunate to have brothers and sisters in the home, normal social heterosexual relationships are something we must work very hard at. I am conscious of a great need here for more activities in which young people of both sexes can participate on the basis of friendship.

Democracy by correspondence

One recent Friday morning a letter arrived at my college which caused some excitement. It was addressed to me and bore the gold crest of the Attorney-General and Minister of Justice of Canada Ray Hnatyshyn.

I had written to him four or five months earlier to express my concerns about a Bill coming before the Canadian Parliament at the time.

His letter began with an apology for having taken four months to reply. He then answered my letter in detail, point by point, in the next five paragraphs. Finally, he thanked me, in closing, for having taken the time to share my concerns with him.

To those who were amazed that he answered my letter, I explained that there is a British tradition, shared by Canada and other Commonwealth countries, of encouraging every citizen's input by allowing postage free letters to members of parliament. This applies to not only your own representative, but to any member. My prime minister also answers. Even if I had written a stupid letter, rather than a carefully researched one, I would at least have received back a brief note, saying, "Thank you for expressing your opinion."

In the United States, such citizen participation in government is equally practised, although it is not "postage free." Many young people in other countries were surprised when the late young Samantha Smith wrote to her president and to the leader of the Soviet Union. I was only surprised that she was an elementary school student, rather than a high school student, whom I would certainly expect to be considering national and international matters.

How different is the reaction in Japan!

Not only do elected members of government not acknowledge their mail, but neither do ministry officials. Before moving to Japan two years ago I wrote to three different senior people at the education ministry, enclosing letters of introduction from my education ministry. One of these letters accompanied a gift of curriculum materials, since the education ministry in Japan had at the time embarked on a major study of curriculum reform. We received no reply, not even a postcard acknowledging the curriculum materials.

This kind of institutional rudeness carries over into business, when young college students send out job applications, complete with official documents. Unless the company wants them, they have no idea whether their letters were received or not. Even after the young person has passed entrance tests and been interviewed, they will be told, "We will call you on (a certain day)." Unless she/he is the successful application, no call comes.

It seems that no one here has heard of such a thing as, "Thank you for your interest in our company, but unfortunately we do not need you at this time. Good luck in finding employment." This minimal courtesy, taken for granted in other industrialized countries, would leave the unsuccessful applicant with a positive feeling towards the company, and soften the disappointment. This aspect of PR is usually neglected by Japanese business.

Thrown to
the lions

Is Japan becoming a nation of masochists and sadists? Like the Roman Empire, at the time when public entertainment consisted of throwing Christians to the lions, and forcing slaves to fight each other, to see which could survive the longest, are we too on the brink of moral decay?

I am forced to examine this question due to the popularity of such a TV program as *Super Jockey* on NTV Sunday afternoons. In it Beat Takeshi and his team of young male masochists endure various forms of torture, for the supposed entertainment of a sadistic audience of home viewers and studio audience.

The studio audience, preponderantly young women who ought to be old enough to know better, are seen applauding their favourite volunteer humiliate himself and cheer when he cries out in pain.

This is **not** simply an extension of the old

stereotypical situation in which boys participate in sports while girls are relegated to the
role of spectator. That, itself is bad enough.

What I am describing is a situation when
cruelty is regarded as funny in a society that is
already worried about the phenomenon of bul-
lying in schools.

To me this is a symptom of something very
sick. That anyone in their right mind would
enjoy public torture either as a participant or
as a spectator defies the imagination, and de-
mands our attention.

The programme, apparently is widely
know about in Canada too, because one of my
Grade Eleven students mentioned it to me in
Ottawa.

Independence for the blind

When I first arrived in Tokyo I was amazed at the fearless manner in which the blind make their way around this large city, navigating the trains and subways somehow without getting killed.

The secret lies in metal panels, embedded down the centre of sidewalks in all the major streets and most minor streets now.

These 10 to 12 inch wide strips are made up of hemispheric bumps about the size of a silver dollar, which the blind can follow with their feet or with their canes. Before you come to a curb, the bumps change to a block of horizontal strips as a warning. These bump-guides turn right into subway and railway stations, and go along the subway platforms at a safe distance from the edge.

A friend also drew my attention to the little speakers attached to the pedestrian walk signals. When the signal changes to "walk", it is accompanied by a little chirpy high-pitched musical sound which also helps to guide the blind across the intersection.

I hope that readers who have visited other parts of the world and have seen different ways in which the needs of the handicapped are met, will write and share these observations, as well as writing with suggestions to our local politicians. This way we can improve living conditions for all of us.

In the Japanese hot bath

I believe I have located the secret to the fine youthful Japanese complexion so may of us admire.

It is due to a devotion to cleanliness, which can extend to a half-hour of soaping, scrubbing and shampooing, followed by soaking for a while in a clean hot bath.

Because of the high cost of heating fuel, which any of you who have ever lived in Nova Scotia will appreciate, the family fills the bath tub once with hot water, and each member of the family takes a turn, when already thoroughly clean, to soak and relax in it. Even after a family of six or seven have taken their turn, it is almost as clean as when the first person entered it.

I'm sure you have all heard the misconceived horror stories of Japanese brides forced to bathe last after all members of their husbands' family have had their turn and imagined some one getting into dirty bath water.

Not at all, it was just not as hot as for the first person, although one is permitted to add more hot water if needed.

For many years I have noticed the excellent complexions of members of swimming and waterpolo teams. You will rarely see a swimmer who does not have a beautiful skin. I believe it is due to the same thing: a thorough daily cleaning of the skin.

No matter what a Japanese girl wears in the way of make up during the day she makes sure it is completely removed at night.

Swimming in Japan

One of my pre-conditions for coming here was that the Tokyo YWCA have a pool. "Why," you may ask. "Don't all Y's have pools?" Sorry, to disappoint you, but in the Orient you can't count on a Y having a pool. Most are for education and cultural programmes only.

In fact, in Ottawa region, our latest Nepean Y-facility in the Nepean Industrial Park (Colonnade Road) does not have a pool, but it has other recreational programmes.

Swimming like every other athletic or leisure activity is very expensive in Japan. It costs Y400 (400 yen) over four dollars compared to one dollar per swimming period at Ottawa's Carlingwood Y, and towel rentals are 100 yen rather than our twenty five cents cost recovery. I have heard of people here being charged up to 3000 or 3500 yen for a single swim in a private club pool or a hotel pool.

Even if you are staying at a first-class hotel with its own pool, don't assume that you are automatically entitled to the use of it as a hotel guest. The hotel will have used attractive photos of their pool as part of their promotional material, and the weather in Tokyo in summer is so hot and damp that you can hardly get your body dry after swimming, because you continue to perspire profusely. Most swimming facilities charge what we would consider exorbitant admission fees.

The swimming periods here are also shorter than I am accustomed to, usually only 45 minutes. Of course there are times, especially on a lunch-hour swim, when one doesn't even have 45 minutes to swim, but it would be really nice to stay longer when we are free to do so.

Something that amazed me here was that for those days when we all had to leave a bit early to go back to work, the life-guard remained on top of her perch for the last five minutes guarding an empty pool. And we could hear, from the shower room, when she blew the whistle at the end of the period, even though there was absolutely no one in the water!

I wrote to one of the local papers, asking about this phenomenon, and was told that the Japanese educational system is such that it does not either nurture or permit individual initiative. It almost seemed to me that she felt her job was to blow her whistle every 45 minutes, rather than to be responsible for people's safety.

I am pleased to be able to report that last week, when we had to leave a bit early, she also left the deck, and we heard no whistle!

A challenge to women

One holiday weekend, I had the pleasure of attending a conference on *The Japanese Women's Place in International Exchange*. The setting, the National Women's Education Centre (Kokuritsu Fujin Kyoiku Kaikan) could not have been more ideal.

The magnitude of the task before us was well presented to the 200 participants from around the world, of all colours and a wide age-range, by Dr. Chie Nakane of Tokyo University, keynote speaker. She began by stating bluntly that Japanese cultural insularity must be overcome, if internationalization is to become more than just a buzzword.

The experience of foreigners here, that after the initial glow of politeness, it is difficult to get to know Japanese people, she attributed to the very closed nature of Japanese society. A good example she gave was the poor acceptance of Vietnamese boat people compared to other countries.

Japanese returnees raised in China, and Japanese students returning after some time spent overseas share the same experience of rejection. She gave the Kansai airport construction project exclusion of other nations, as another example of Japanese prejudice or exclusiveness. How did these characteristics develop?

One of the factors she identified was physical isolation from other cultures. People spent their entire lives in their own villages, so isolated that in the Edo, or Tokugawa period warriors from Kagoshima couldn't understand the dialect of warriors from Kansai. They had grown up thinking everyone was the same. Even Japanese people from different social classes or different villages didn't mix.

While in China there is an awareness of other people's cultural differences, she said that even today most Japanese people have no experience with foreigners, and so try to avoid them.

Japanese society was not always so closed, however. Even up to the mid-Edo period, she pointed out that Korean craftsmen and Korean poets were welcome. The characteristic exclusiveness developed during the Edo period. This closed mentality must be overcome, and we must begin to appreciate differences, we were told.

Nakane believes that Japanese women hold the key to such changes. She finds Japanese women to be much more receptive to change and more adaptable than Japanese men. A good illustration of this might be that women generally look at the spirit of a law, that is, its intent, whereas most men might look at the letter of the law, and not always with the intention of respecting it. I can support this latter observation in the case of the Equal Employment Opportunity Law, when many Japanese businessmen were chiefly interested in how to circumvent the law, not how to implement it.

She pointed out that some Japanese have found that they can have closer friendships with foreigners that they can have with other Japanese. She spoke with some nostalgia for her own experience in Britain where she could have true friends with foreigners, both men and women.

Finally she challenged us with this statement, "Don't create barriers by saying that Japanese culture is too hard to understand. Different cultures need not create barriers to understanding."

Following Dr. Nakane's address, we heard a multinational, multiracial panel of wives and mothers who had spent from five years to most of their lives in Japan.

Eva Katedze, wife of the ambassador from Zimbabwe, who is a former college lecturer and whose family had also spent some years in the United States, pointed out that most Japanese children don't play with foreign children. She called for mothers to encourage children to visit and play in each others homes.

Miyo Chen, born and educated in Japan, of Chinese ancestry, spent over 15 years in the United States and United Kingdom before returning to Japan where her husband is now a Todai professor. She raised the painful subject of the prevalent attitudes in Japan toward Asian women.

Ruri Kawashima, also born and educated in Japan, has spent 15 years in the United States. She observed that experts and professionals seemed able to accept each other, but the major difficulty lay with ordinary people in not making an effort to receive foreigners.

For the final half-day we divided into three sections, one of which took part in Japanese food preparation. Another group dealt with exchange activities between Asian and African women, and a third discussed the conditions affecting Japanese women from the perspective of a lawyer. She pointed to some of the good changes in Japanese law such as the fairly recent (1985) provision for Japanese mothers to confer their citizenship on their children, equally with fathers. She also indicated some blatant inequities such as the fact that after a divorce, a man may remarry immediately, while a woman is forced to wait six months. Unequal division of property after a divorce is still most common, rather than an exception.

I shared my concern that as long as only seven percent of the Japanese population travels abroad each year, and half of those go only as tourists or on business, it is almost impossible for them to learn about the customs, values and life styles of people in other countries. It is only by homestays and close friendships in other countries that we gain a deep appreciation for each other's perspective.

Another member mentioned problems experienced by people in cultures in which both parents have careers, such as in China, when one parent is transferred and the other is unable to follow. Severe pressures on such families contribute to stress, marital infidelity and marriage breakdown.

This is closely paralleled in Japan in families in which a father may be transferred to another city, and the family unable to accompany him because of the very restrictive entrance examination system.

Among the most valuable results of this conference was the exchange of information about existing groups and services.

Two such services are located at the Tokyo YWCA. *Japanese Mothers For Foreign Students* founded in 1961, provides counselling, welcome and foster parenting but does not yet include homestays. One of the first career counselling and job placement offices in Japan is also located here, and is a free-of-charge service to all women. It operates with national government funding.

We really needed another half-day to reach some conclusions, make resolutions and recommendations. One participant pointed out that we were the fortunate women who could afford both the time and the money to attend such an international meeting, while most women could afford neither.

I would hope that the next such conference would find a way to offer scholarship help and provide child-care, so that an even wider group of women could be represented.

Sumo buff

Many young Japanese tell me they find sumo boring. My younger son and I, however, have been hooked on sumo for nearly four years.

In the New Year's tournament I had to the great pleasure of witnessing sumo "live" for the first time.

While at first, to be honest, my interest was simply a matter of vanity. My children had thoughtfully informed me that I was the only member of the family with the required natural build to be a sumo wrestler. (One's children can usually be relied upon for such tactful comments.) Only a sumo wrestler could make one feel like the Princess of Wales, by contrast.

As a person involved in other sports, I was soon engrossed in the combination of strength, agility and weight needed for success in this sport.

The ability of some comparatively light wrestler about 200 pounds, to overcome opponents more than twice their size, say about

500 pounds, is certainly exciting. Some of the moves are similar to judo or karate, in fact, but are called by other names.

Having been involved as a coach of young men's and women's swimming and water polo teams for nearly 20 years, I am also impressed by the evidences of sportsmanship I see when some wrestlers put out a hand to keep an opponent from falling off the dohyo or help him up after he has been defeated.

Several of my favourites have recently retired, high-lighting the short professional career span of this sport, even shorter than professional baseball or hockey.

While I admire the agility of the superheavyweights, I cannot help being anxious about the effects of such excess weight on health and life-span. Because of this concern, I cannot fully share the enjoyment felt by older Japanese in watching the classical sumo shape.

Many sumo fans were deeply disappointed in the premature termination of Futahaguro's career. It seems that he could not cope with the changes in working conditions for the lowest level of "stable hands" from the time that he was one himself.

Such inflexibility afflicts many older Japanese and contributes largely to the generation gap we observe here. What a tragedy to see a man in his early 20s suffering from the same kind of inflexibility toward his juniors!

Even if your interest is very superficial, you cannot help admiring Chiyonofji, a recent, long-reigning grand champion. Though he once had very serious upper arm injuries requiring surgery, he appears to have recovered completely, and represents the finest in masculine beauty.

Sumo is more than entertainment. It has become my addiction.

Common interest

One recent summer one of my former students from Tokyo visited me in Ottawa, at the time of our annual jazz festival. On her second evening here, my son and I, and an older friend of mine, took our visitor to a jazz bar for the evening. She was really surprised to see such a wide range in age among the audience, from teenagers to octogenarians. "It's so nice," she said, "to see so many older people out having a good time."

She saw what I meant when I had told her that in Canada we choose our friends on the basis of common interests, without regard to age. In fact there are many good friends whose age I don't really know, and would not think of asking.

Oh Omiai!

During my last stay in Japan I was asked to comment on the strengths and weaknesses of *omiai* (arranged marriages) method of selecting a marriage partner. I replied after my initial shock at the concept, I could see several strengths in it which I would like to explore here.

The most important strength, I feel,lies in the fact that if two families have shared in the responsibility of helping choose marriage partners, they continue to bear a responsibility for the success of the marriage, to help in time of difficulty and resolve misunderstandings. If you have a wise "go-between," this person also feels such a responsibility, and can advise the young people before a problem explodes into a crisis.

This contrasts with the practice in Canada where families are so spread across the country that they may be thousands of miles apart. One might not even meet one's in-laws before the wedding itself, and sometimes only infrequently afterwards. In my own case, my mother and father-in-law lived three thousand mile away. Even though I was psychologically and emotionally closer to them than to my own parents, I could never worry them about problems about which they were too far away to do anything.

Rather than being supportive toward young people's marriages, some parents in North America are divisive, telling their children that the person they married is "not good enough" for them. No wonder there is such a high failure rate in such marriages!

In Canada over ten percent of women suffer physical abuse at the hands of their partners. There are also a few cases of husbands abused by their wives. Some of these violent cases lead to the death of the victim. No family member or neighbour has intervened. We have too much privacy.

In Japan, in the family of one of my close friends, in a similar situation, the wife's relatives confronted the abusive husband. He had repeatedly attacked his wife, until she was obliged to flee from the house on several occasions.

When it was clear to him that his wife's family would not tolerate his behaviour, he signed a written agreement in which he promised his wife sole ownership of their house and exclusive rights to their life savings if he lost control of himself again. Since them, there have been no more incidents, over a period of years. We need this kind of "interfering relatives!"

A second strength I see in Omiai, is the fact that both young people know that each other's intentions are honourable, that is, that both parties have marriage in mind. Having this fact plain from the outset could save a great deal of misunderstanding and suffering, such as in cases where people go out together exclusively for a long time, up to two or three years. One of the pair may assume that marriage will be the outcome, while the other does not want any such responsibilities.

One of my concerns about Omiai has to do with the qualities sought, particularly with respect to the young man. Too frequently the brides' family are overly concerned with his education and place of employment.

This would be most inappropriate in Canada, because highly intelligent upwardly mobile people frequently return to university as adults, improving their career situation. In fact up to one third of Canadian university students are adults. On the other hand, one's employer could also go bankrupt, leaving the employees on their own to locate another job, possibly after several months' search. Both education and employment can change.

It seems to me that the most important characteristics to be sought in a marriage partner are strength of character, and interesting personality, a sense of humour, and thoughtfulness of others. Who would want to spend their life with an intelligent, well-educated narcissist?

Another weakness is that some people choose their supervisor at work to be the "go-between," rather than a good family friend. The disadvantage here is that the wife would not feel free to discuss a family problem with her husband's boss, fearing to appear disloyal or to jeopardize his chances of advancement. I would not want to discuss personnel matters with my own boss because I would feel that he or she already knew too much about me, and it would destroy any shred of privacy I might have.

Omiai is a good system provided the young people are not pressured into making a decision too quickly. Time is needed to assess an individual's personal strengths,and to reveal such problems as alcoholism which could destroy the marriage later. The commitment on the part of both families to the success of their children's marriage is the most significant value of all.

About divorce

Does Canada have a serious divorce problem? That was the question I was recently asked by a serious scholar of Japanese social problems. I believe he was asking the wrong question. Divorce is a symptom of many problems, a measure of other problems, and a solution to some of them.

Divorce itself is a "fact," not a "problem" although some governments like that of Ireland choose to pretend that if they make divorce impossible, the other problems will disappear.

Some family problems include wife abuse (a minimum of one in ten Canadian families), alcoholism a serious problem in many homes, child abuse we are becoming increasingly aware of.

Many couples married for the wrong reasons, such as women who got married to escape an unhappy parental home, or to have "someone take care of them," or men who wanted an ornament or a possession rather than a partner with her own feelings and needs.

Some people become so alienated from each other that hostility reaches a damaging level for themselves and also for their children, even if they try to hide the situation from their children.

Marriage should not include such "life sentences" in civilized society.

In the past, many conditions which used to prevent divorce even when it was warranted included lack of support systems for abuse victims. Formerly women's total economic dependence on men, meant that they could not take care of themselves and their children no matter how bad their circumstances were.

The number of such "life sentences" has thankfully been reduced.

I see hopeful signs in Canadian society leading to a decreasing divorce rate in the future.

First, I feel we have passed through the era of the "throw-away" mentality. When the car or the refrigerator, or some other appliance broke down we did not try to repair it. We threw it out and got a new one.

In my opinion this led to a carry over into human relationships, and some people did not work hard enough at making marriage successful.

Other hopeful signs are that young people are making more thoughtful decisions about marriage partners, centring on friendship and mutual respect. effective birth control has reduced the number of "forced marriages."

Many people choose not to marry at all, since the old social pressures and stigma toward unmarried people has nearly disappeared.

Japanese
funerals

Twice, during my stay in Japan, I have attended funerals, once as an "acting" relative. Like the Irish, a wake is the custom, for two or three days in the home of the deceased, or if they have no home, at the funeral parlour.

The funeral service itself was conducted by a Buddhist priest. During the service we all went up and lit incense at the front of the funeral chapel. In one case, we each dropped a flower into the casket before the cremation.

In Japan we must all be cremated, as there is not enough room for burial. Most families have their own small space in a local cemetery where many family members' ashes are placed.

Cremation is at a lower temperature than in North America, so the bones are not completely turned to ashes. Immediate family or very close friends use long chopsticks and working in pairs, place the bones into the urn and then the ashes are added. Following the ceremony cagefulls of white doves are set free to symbolize the rising of the spirit of the deceased.

Memorial services are held on the 49th day when the ashes are interred, one year later, three, and again seven years later.

Because funerals are so expensive, those who attend are expected to bring money and, in fact, a relative has the responsibility of sitting near the door as people arrive and listing the names and, something we would consider in poor taste, the amount of the donation beside the donor's name.

As guests leave they are given a gift bag with a white handkerchief to wave good-bye to the deceased and a small packet of salt to wash away evil, and a bottle of *sake*, although sometimes other gifts are included.

At a Japanese
wedding

I had the honour of participating in the wedding of a young relative while I lived in Tokyo. The bride was the grand-daughter of my step-mother-in-law. (I am one of those lucky people to have had two great mothers-in-law.)

The wedding took place in the bride's father's church, there being Protestant clergymen for generations on both sides of her family. Although Christians number only one percent of the population, more and more young people in Japan today are opting for a Christian wedding ceremony.

After the wedding all the relatives on both sides of the family withdrew to a small reception room. There, a senior member of each side stood up and introduced every member of his or her side of the family to the other side, telling a bit about each one.

From the church the whole party moved on to a hotel for the reception dinner with their closest friends. The bride and groom changed into formal wedding Kimono. At a very formal wedding, they would change two or three times, with photos being taken in each set of garments.

In a more traditional family the wedding ceremony would be performed by a Shinto priest. Or they might have two wedding ceremonies.

During the reception a "candle light service" takes place. This is not a worship service as we might expect, but involves the newly-weds going from table to table among their relatives and friends with a lighted candle, with which they light the candles on each table in the room.

Wedding receptions in hotels have become so expensive these days that it has become the unhappy practise to invite only one member of each guest family, usually the senior male member, to the wedding reception.

That way you are sure to get the gift, usually cash, and not have to feed the whole clan.

A Canadian born friend of mine whose wife is Japanese, and living over there, had such an experience. One of his wife's girlfriends got married, and he was the only member of their household to be invited.

Both of her parents being deceased, he was considered the "head" of the family. He hardly knew the bridal couple.

He felt it would have been much more appropriate to have had either his wife or her sister, both of whom knew the bride well, represent their family.

Ethnocentrism

Last week a Japanese friend whom I have known for may years asked me why I became involved with the civil rights movement, in the 1960's, during the eight-year period that our family lived in the United States.

"Was it for the excitement?" he asked.

For a moment I was speechless. This person knows we are an interracial family and has met one of my children. Ignorance and cruelty seemed out of character for him. However, since the Japanese are such an overwhelming majority in Japan, where only approximately 1 percent of the population are immigrants, it simply did not occur to him that Japanese would be a minority in Canada and the United States.

It did not cross his mind that Japanese-Canadians might have experienced some of the discrimination felt by other minorities, including problems with housing and teasing of one's children. Violence could even have been part of the experience, as in the case of a Japanese-American friend of ours who was attacked on the street by a total stranger, who knocked his teeth out.

At the time I was also teaching in a 97-percent black school in Buffalo, N.Y., and as civil rights problems involved my daily life, it was quite a logical interest for me.

"Yes," I agreed. "It was exciting. You met all the best people! One thing I must say about that kind of experience is that it either brings out the best in a person, or else it destroys them."

My friend was suffering from the same problem of ethnocentrism that English-speaking tourists did, years ago, when they went abroad with the attitude that all the other people were the "foreigners."

Similarly, some American tourists enter Canada and Japan carrying guns, and are outraged when these weapons are confiscated. Their attitude is the same one expressed by the spokesman of the (U.S.) National Rifle Association, Paul Blackman, when he says, "I don't think Americans should have to obey Canadian (or Japanese) laws." This is not respect for law.

Here, in this country of contradictions, I have met both the genuine politeness for which Japan is noted, but also some totally unexpected rudeness. While most people behave toward others with incredible kindness, side-by-side with it you can also find unbelievable cruelty. All too frequently we read cases where schoolchildren here are tormented into suicide by classmates who have deeply-rooted prejudice against anyone who seems "different."

While it may be partly explained by their lack of experience with those who are truly different, this is an attitude which Japan must overcome, if it is ever to become a genuinely international country.

A foreign journalist in Tokyo recently went so far as to say that since minorities in Japan are so few in number, it doesn't matter what the Japanese do to them. He does not realize that he, himself, is part of the minority!

I, for one, endorse the statement of Pope John Paul II, made on his 1987 North American tour, when he said that the measure of civilization lies in how it treats its weakest members, its poor, its sick, and its minorities.

It is vital that Japan not fail in this measure of its culture.

After the Ninth

Recently, a good friend of mine had an expensive experience with a dead cat. It wasn't even his dead cat! It just happened by, and expired in his back yard.

Unlike most other parts of Japan, and unlike most parts of Canada, Tokyo does not permit the burial of a pet in one's own back yard or in a field. You cannot even slip the stiff into your garbage. A Tokyo city by-law requires you to take the body to the office of the local ward, an area about the same size as one of our postal districts. There for a fee of about Y2,000 they will dispose of it for you, presumably by cremation, which is also compulsory for human remains.

Unfortunately, this friend is a chronically under-employed part-time teacher who could not afford to keep a live cat. To add insult to injury, since he has no car, he had to carry the body on the train and the subway to the district office.

Japan is an expensive country to die in, whether you are a person or a pet.

Working
conditions
for women

Since 1977 Canada has had legislation guaranteeing equality in the workplace, yet even today, full-time employed Canadian woman earn, on an average, only about seventy percent as much as the average man. Prejudices and stereotypes still exist.

Discrimination dies slowly. Sometimes parents and schools are at fault for not sufficiently encouraging their talented girls.

I recall my experience in the early 1950's as an actuarial trainee with the head office of a large insurance company. My employers refused to prepare me for the higher math examinations, and only offered me half of the normal salary.

Their excuse was that female employees were a poor investment. Even then, over thirty years ago, their own personnel department could have proved to them that their women showed greater company loyalty, as measured by a lower rate of staff turnover than their male employees, and would thus have been the better investment.

It is with great interest and concern that I will be watching to see how the new equal employment legislation in Japan will be implemented.

Since 1977 we have had, in Canada, none of the old "protective" legislation. In previous centuries it was introduced to meet a genuine need, to prevent women from being unduly exploited by working extraordinarily long hours, and in dangerous conditions at much lower pay.

Now our men and women are protected by the same legislation. For example, employers who require more than 48 hours' work in a given week must obtain a permit from the ministry of labour, and all hours in excess of 44 hours a week must be paid for at "time-and-a-half" rate.

I am particularly worried that, in Japan, these old "protective" laws related to female employment have not been rescinded. As long as these laws exist they will serve as an excuse for discrimination. If women may not be employed after certain hours an employer will pass over a deserving female candidate for a supervisory position. The new equal access legislation will be impossible to implement.

Another distressing remnant of the past is something in Japan called "menstrual leave." Now I would be the first to admit that probably the origins of "sick leave" stemmed from a way to provide for women in such circumstances. However, we have "sick leave" equally for men and women in Canada, and standard practice is for twenty days a year paid sick leave in all our contracts.

I think it is significant that last year a major study in U.S. industry showed that women lost an average of 1.3 days per year in menstrual related illness. A little over one day per year is surely a very minor matter.

U.S. employers also cited advantages in hiring women because they had fewer alcohol and drug-related problems than male employees.

In Canada we share the U.S. experience that women take more short sick leaves of a day or two, but that men take longer sick leave because they tend to neglect themselves until they are in a much worse condition.

As a competitive swimmer from the age of 13, I was obliged to train and compete as a team member, 365 days a year, including my years on Canada's National Team.

I would not tell my own grandmother when I was having my "period" and certainly not my boss! I think it is shockingly embarrassing that "menstrual leave" exists in Japan. We cannot simultaneously have equality and inequality in the workplace.

Something must be done to resolve this situation.

Pension irritant

One of the biggest difficulties encountered by those who spend part of their working life in Japan is the lack of reciprocal pension agreements between Japan and other countries.

Canada has such agreements with the U.S., most of Europe, and many Caribbean nations, 24 in all, whereby if a person works ten or more years in two of these, she/he may claim a part-pension from both countries.

In Japan pensions are not portable. A man must be employed by the same company for at least 20 years to be eligible, and a surviving spouse has to have remained married to the man during these same years. Foreign employees in Japan rarely work that long, and so lose all their Japanese pension benefits.

If Japan is serious about becoming "international" a good first step would be to enter into such reciprocal pension agreements with the U.S. and Canada, for starters. It would certainly relieve the resentment may foreigners feel to see compulsory pension deductions, from which they cannot hope to benefit.

Sexism, misinterpreted

According to Shogakkan's *Progressive English-Japanese Dictionary*, published in Showa 55 (1980), sexism is defined as a) prejudice, or b) discrimination, especially in occupation or political areas.

If we recognize sexism as undesirable and wish to reduce or eliminate it, we must know what it is, marshall our resources against it, not simply apply a series of "band-aids" to its symptoms.

Sexism leads to discrimination based solely on sex, in the same way that racism leads to discrimination based solely on colour. In many societies it is supported by social custom, and in some countries it is enforced by law.

In some Middle East countries, Saudi Arabia for example, it is illegal for females to drive a car.

In many countries, in some periods in their history, property ownership was a criterion for being an elector, and as long as women were not allowed to own property they were totally disenfranchised.

One of the symptoms of sexism is a salary differential in favour of male employees. This is a reflection of the idea that the work done by women is of less value.

Legislation can be helpful, in the form of equal pay for equal work laws, and equal value laws, introduced in industrialized countries at various times in the second half of this century.

Laws alone, however, cannot remove sexist attitudes.

When the Equal Employment Opportunity law was enacted in Japan in May 1986, many companies, rather than try to implement the law, looked for ways to avoid compliance with it. One major company decided to consider women for promotion at age thirty-one, compared to age twenty-three for men, and did not recognize this as blatant discrimination. Another company hired a teaching colleague of mine to design a difficult written test, which would be given to female candidates only. It will be worth while to see just how effective this piece of legislation has been, after another five years experience.

Sexism can be fatal. If you were a female

infant in China during the one child per family era, your family might decide to terminate you, on the chance of having a male baby next time. The shortsightedness of this policy will only be fully recognized a generation later when a surplus of unmarried males may lobby to import brides. In many Third World countries, low supplies of food lead to deprivation of female children first, causing permanent health and development damage.

Sexism is not only measured in terms of political and civil rights. What we are faced with is the attitude that women and men are so different that they should fulfil totally different roles in society.

Even though this was thoroughly disputed by an international conference of physicians in the mid-1980's, who concluded that there was less than three percent difference structurally and functionally between men and women, this notion is very deep-rooted.

At homes and schools sexist attitudes must be recognized and challenged.

Sexist males had mothers as well as fathers, and many studies in different countries have shown that the attitudes of mothers have a greater influence on children than their fathers' attitudes.

Sexism is very widely misunderstood. The

most shocking to me of these false impressions was one expressed by a middle aged Japanese male, university graduate, who insisted that sexism can make women pregnant! This would be a little difficult, since sexism is essentially a matter of attitudes, and does not involve body contact. It appears that he was confusing sexism with what is known in English-speaking countries as "wife abuse", although even in the latter case over seventy-five percent of wife abuse takes the form of psychological abuse. Another portion consists of sheer physical abuse such as beating and only a small fraction takes any form which might cause pregnancy.

It is entirely possible, for example for a country to be comparatively non-violent and yet relatively sexist. In the same way it is possible for a country to be rather violent, and yet almost entirely non-sexist. These are two separate problems with little if anything in common, and require two entirely different concentrated approaches to eliminate them.

About
Mr. Clean

Y ou have already heard me on the subject of how fanatically clean the
Japanese are. They scrub a layer of skin off
their own bodies and vacuum and dust their
small abodes from stem to stern everyday, but
their car care really takes the cake.

By now, I am accustomed to the upholstery
of cars being protected by seat covers that re-
semble large lace doilies that cover at least the
top half of the seat, and the head-rest completely.

I doubt, however, if I can ever pass by,
without a chuckle, when I see mature men, on
the street in the morning, dusting the outside
of their cars with long feather dusters. These
are long enough to reach half of the car, from
one side. Then they go around to the other
side to do that half.

One of my students described for me how
hard her father tried to keep his new blue se-
dan in mint condition... so hard that he had

worn through the paint in several places in less than a year.

She and I spent sometime doubled up in laughter, as she told me about it. She had had to stifle the temptation to giggle, on the weekend at her father's consternation. Now we know it is possible to be **too clean.**

Green tea break

Which do you prefer coffee, black tea or green tea? And which do you drink most often? Did you know that green tea is one of nature's finest sources of vitamin C? I was surprised to learn that the finest quality green tea is judged both on its taste and on its vitamin content.

Green tea has played a very important role in the health of Japan's population. Fresh fruit is not eaten so freely here, partly due to the high cost and partly due to habit.

As a result, as coffee has become more popular here in the last 10 to 20 years, especially among teenagers and young working people, a significant vitamin C deficiency has developed.

Here we can see vividly illustrated the kind of unexpected problem that can arise when a diet item of one culture is adopted by another. It reminds me a little of the health problems created when powdered milk formula was promoted for babies in Third World countries, where clean water was not available resulting in fatal consequences.

Did you know that green tea has been found to reduce the chances of developing cancer? Neither tannin nor caffeine, common to black tea and coffee, have been found responsible for countering cancer. It is something peculiar to green tea. This may be why it also reduces significantly the effects of nuclear fallout containing radioactive cesium and strontium, such as we experienced after the Chernobyl accident.

Green tea also helps prevent high blood pressure, thus serving to counteract the very high salt content of the typical Japanese diet.

Black tea and coffee are no nutritional match for green tea. It not only tastes good and smells good, it's good for you. Let's have a "green tea break!"

Beware the
Japanese egg

Perhaps the Japanese have been successful in completely eliminating salmo-
nella organisms in poultry and eggs. Since
other kinds of food poisoning do occasionally
take place, I am not confident of this, and am
very concerned about the careless handling of
eggs in this country.

A colleague of mine was recently invited
on a home stay. She was distressed on the first
morning of her visit, when she got up about
seven o'clock, to find that her host had got up
around four and the first thing he had done
was fry an egg for her. It had been on the plate
all that time and was very unappetizing.

Another friend of mine attended a conference at a small hotel. To get to the bathroom
in the middle of the night, she had to pass the
dining-room. The door was open, she was
rather shocked to look in and see a hundred
eggs, all fried and served on each plate. She
had no idea how long they had been there, and
wondered if it had been the cook's last act, the

previous night, before going home to bed!

Next morning her roommate said cheerfully, "I wonder what's for breakfast?" My friend replied, "I know, I saw it last night".

A common inexpensive portable lunch carried by both school children and workmen is a plastic container with cold steamed rice and a cold fried egg prepared at breakfast time. It is jokingly referred to as a "rising sun" lunch.

In this country eggs are sometimes served when in Canada we might have judged them unsafe and thrown them out.

It is both safer and much more enjoyable in Japan to order a Japanese style breakfast. That usually consists of soup, steamed rice, sometimes a tasty rice porridge, vegetables, salad and tea.

Apart from the rice-porridge, there is nothing really to distinguish a traditional Japanese breakfast from the other meals of the day.

Going to
the dentist

One of the students in my most advanced class non-credit English course was a professor of dentistry, who became not only my student, but my dentist, and my friend.

I had been in Japan about a year, and had thus missed two of my regular six-month check ups at home, when I asked him for an appointment. He asked if anything hurt me, and I said "No," and went on to explain our custom of preventative dentistry in Canada. As it happened, a couple of days before my appointment, one of my caps came loose, and when I was checked my other cap also needed to be replaced.

I was pleased to find that dentistry in Japan is covered under the same medical insurance plan — ninety percent was covered, ten percent was due up front. But interestingly, that only applied to the labour. Material used was billed separately and was not covered.

Obstructing nose

Twice a year I go for an eye examination and glaucoma check-up. I went to an eye clinic and was given a test in which a tiny light approached you on various sides and you were to tell when you saw it.

"You have the beginning of glaucoma," said the doctor. "Your eye pressure is normal now, but come back in three months."

Three months later, I was told there was no change, but to come back in six months this time. So I did, but this time I asked to see the chart showing my narrowed range of vision. It fell in an outline on either side of my nose.

I pointed this out to the doctor and told him I couldn't see the little light there, since my nose was in the way! "I think you're right, I made a mistake." It is very uncommon and gracious of a Japanese doctor to say so. All of his other patients had noses with low bridges, and as a result very few Japanese can see their own nose (without a mirror).

Interesting that this standard vision test could not be used with me.

Environmental responsibility

Recently a group of Japanese young people asked me to comment on environmental protection. I believe that manufacturers must be responsible for the cost of any resulting environmental damage. If this makes their goods very expensive then we should know their true costs and decide for ourselves whether to use them.

We must also pass laws preventing us from causing environmental damage to the third world countries.

I was pleased, a couple of months ago, to read that the Japanese Ministry of Science and Technology had informed Japanese companies that they must respect the same standards of radiation safety when working overseas as they do at home.

We must expand this to all chemical and biological safety as well as radioactive materials. If all industrialized nations do not take such responsibility, it may be necessary to take it to the international level in a forum such as the United Nations.

Because we who live in industrialized countries cause 20 times as much damage to the environment as do those in the Third World countries, we are much more dangerous to the planet and require much more strict regulation.

Help from the homeless

On my last assignment in Japan my work took me once a week to an area near the Tokyo Railway Station. Below the station is an underground shopping centre extending two or three blocks beyond the station building and ending in subterranean tunnels for pedestrians to cross the busy streets.

One day I paused in one of these tunnels and asked two homeless men, sitting on spread-out newspapers, with their belongings beside them: *Sumimasen ... Tokyo eki no iriguchi wa dochira desuka*? (Excuse me, which way is the entrance to Tokyo Station?)

One of them jumped up and, in his sock feet, ran down the corridor, indicating the right way. Friends I was staying with commented that I must have been the only person, other than the police telling them to move along, to speak to them for some time. I think they were pleased to be spoken to, and not as if they were human garbage.

Liberators

One of the things that surprised and at first puzzled me in Japan was their strong affection for Americans. The closest thing I have experienced to this myself were the warm feelings expressed by the Dutch toward Canadians, following their liberation by Canadians in World War II. I felt this warmth when I went to summer school in Holland in 1980.

In discussion with Japanese in their 40's and 50's, I found that they regarded the Americans as liberators as they had been expecting a harsh or brutal occupation, and were overjoyed and grateful that it was not. I had been expecting resentment on the part of an "occupied country."

I worry very much about those thoughtless politicians and business people who "Japan bash" or "U.S. bash," lest they damage this great reservoir of good feeling.

When in Rome...

Japanese tourists, I find, are not properly counselled about certain important Western customs. Ignorance about these can bring your North American visit to an abrupt and embarrassing end.

Take, for example, being drunk in a public place. Did you know that in British Columbia, the Canadian province, where the largest number of Japanese tourists go, if you are convicted of this offence you could be subject to a penalty of $2,000 or six months in jail?

Public intoxication is regarded as a serious offence in every province except Manitoba.

Another, and somewhat related problem is the practice of some Japanese males, of "going to the toilet" outdoors in a public place.

This crime is referred to as "public exposure" and in Toronto you could be shot for it!

Last year a Toronto policeman shot a neighbour who had this annoying habit of using the bushes between their properties.

No charges for the shooting were brought against the police officer, who said that he "thought there was a prowler in the yard."

Knowing such things in advance can help assure a safe and enjoyable vacation.

Travel agents must overcome their embarrassment and counsel their clients frankly.

Baby,
it's cold inside

A few months ago a couple of young friends of mine were transferred to Japan for a two year term. As they were expecting their first child in a few months, I tried to alert them about the severe cold indoors in Japan in winter. I told them about the lack of central heating, absence of insulation, and that windows are single-pane and often so loose that they rattle!

I had the opportunity to visit them before Christmas, and they conceded that I had been right. They were trying to keep warm with an electric space heater mounted on the wall, near the ceiling, while their baby lay on a pile of blankets in the middle of the floor.

Now they understand why I wore Shetland wool sweaters indoors all winter in Japan, at home or at work, something I would never have to do in Canada.

Weather words

One miserable February morning my Japanese language teacher asked, *Ii tenki desuka*? It was one of those bitterly cold Ottawa winter mornings when you're not quite sure your car will start. In fact some of my classmates didn't make it to school that morning, through a combination of bitter wind and drifting of the previous day's snowfall.

I looked at my teacher in surprise and said, *Iie, taihen samui desu shi kaze ga arimasu, ii tenki dewa arimaren.* She said I was wrong.

We found that our problem was in the translation. We had been taught that *ii tenki* meant good or fine weather, whereas Japanese really mean clear weather. I discussed this recently with some Japanese friends who said, "Perhaps it's a different perspective. We think about it from the viewpoint of the sky, while your culture sees it from the viewpoint of people!" My answer, that because of the cold and strong wind the weather wasn't nice, was wrong from the viewpoint of my teacher. Another interesting cultural difference.

Dangerous
half truth

A young friend of mine, recently married, went to her doctor to ask for advice regarding birth control. He warned her that because she has a mild heart condition, she ought not to use birth control pills as they might be dangerous to her health.

It was what he failed to tell her, however, that could have been fatal. He did not tell her that a pregnancy would be more dangerous, or that even an early term abortion would be more dangerous than using the Pill.

The side effects he described only occurred with early, experimental high-hormone dosage birth control pills when they first came on the market well over 20 years ago. The improved low-dosage hormone pills now available in most other countries have practically eliminated such side effects, and reduced them to a level where their use is a sensible choice.

Can it be that the medical community in Japan is nearly as ill-informed in this matter as the general public?

Do it
my way

While I was living in my college dormitory in Tokyo, one of my teaching colleagues, originally from England, came over for supper. She was shocked to see the girls in our residence washing the dishes with lukewarm water, and drying them with soon-to-become damp tea towels.

I told her that coughs and colds spread wildly through our house. We discussed the fact that such casual dishwashing practices would be illegal in her country and mine.

Since we were seated at tables for four, and each table group was responsible for washing its own dishes, I soon developed the habit of shooing the students away and doing them single handed. When the girls tried to help me, they always turned down the water temperature, which had the effect of giving any germs an invigorating bath.

Resisting
change

I had an interesting but frustrating experience last year trying to get a Canadian Rotary International student into any of half a dozen Japanese universities.

While the Japanese government seems to be encouraging openness and internationalization the universities are strongly resisting. It takes a least two years to process these applications. At the urging of the Rotary International Scholarship Committee I made initial contacts with the five universities selected on the student's application. I requested in English, accompanied by a correct formal Japanese translation, a catalogue which lists the courses offered in each year. We needed these in order to judge whether the student's undergraduate courses matched properly. We already had such a book from Sophia (Jochi Daigaku) University which the student had previously attended for a summer session.

The universities resisted either by giving

wrong or irrelevant answers to our request. One university replied that their entrance exams for this year were already past. This was not our question, since we were looking two years into the future. Another, Saitama University, asked for money, and then sent the wrong thing! The Tokyo Institute of Technology replied that they only take foreign students if they have a faculty member who knows one of the student's professors. The student came from a small but excellent university where his professors know not a single Japanese, and certainly not a faculty member at the Tokyo Institute. This policy would cut out most students around the world. The only university which sent information requested and a contact name, was Hosei University.

In frustration, I wrote to a person in Japan whom I was told had some responsibility for Rotary scholars. I asked whether that person's experience would indicate if there were some Japanese universities more receptive to foreign students. All I got was the one-sentence reply, "We are only responsible for foreign students once they arrive in Japan."

Clearly, if we are to have successful exchange of students, we need an effective system of information exchange, and a genuine commitment by Japanese universities to the project.